# indian

NEW
HOLLAND

# contents

Indian dishes ........................................................ 5

Spices, mixes and blends ........................................... 11

Side dishes ........................................................ 21

Vegetarian ........................................................ 59

Poultry ........................................................ 101

Meat ........................................................ 133

Seafood ........................................................ 161

Desserts ........................................................ 177

Index ........................................................ 190

# Indian dishes

*Indian cuisine is often categorized into four food regions. A more refined breakdown reveals that there are eight distinct areas, all with unique food histories and divergent tastes. Knowledge of each of the regions of India will help you understand the vast array of flavours and food in this vibrant cuisine.*

## North India

The hearty food of the north has Muslim and Moghul influences, resulting in a variety of savoury, rich lamb and goat dishes based on cooking with ghee and cream. The cuisine is further enhanced by the tandoor method of cooking, which was indigenous to the north-west frontier, now the Punjab and Pakistan. The tandoor (clay oven), which burns wood or charcoal, imparts an unparalleled smoky flavour to mildly spiced, tender meats and poultry, fish and breads. Punjabi food is simple and filling, an amalgamation of the cuisines of the Greeks, Persians, Afghans, Moghuls and northern invaders.

## Maharashtra

The people of Maharashtra, of which Mumbai is the capital, prepare healthy food with an emphasis on rice, vegetables (as Maharashtrians are generally vegetarians), nuts and nut oils. Often vegetables are spiced with a combination of ground and roasted cumin seeds, sesame seeds, cardamom, cinnamon and coconut. Sweet and sour dishes make for tantalising eating.

## Gujarat

From Maharashtra's neighbouring state of Gujarat comes an interesting vegetarian cuisine called thali. The food is oil-free and thali restaurant waiters will refill your bowls until you are full. Thali has become an institution in India's major cities. Gujarati are fond of relishes and pickles.

## Sindh

The Sindhis migrated to India after the 1947 partition, bringing with them a cuisine characterised by garlic, mint-flavoured chutneys, pickles and very sweet meats. Sindhi food is not necessarily vegetarian. An example is kofta tas-me. These are meatballs served in a sauce of onion, tomato, chilli, ginger and coriander (cilantro), and sprinkled with garam masala.

## Parsi

Like Christians, the Parsis have no religious dietary restrictions. Their cuisine is not overly hot, so it is a favourite with many foreigners. Traditionally, on Sunday, Parsis (most of whom live in Mumbai) add several dhals to meat and chicken and serve them with caramelised brown rice.

## Bengal

Freshwater and saltwater fish, seafood and the flavour of mustard seed dominate the Bengali diet. Fish is grilled (broiled), fried or stewed. Yogurt is offered separately and is sometimes also used in cooking. Bengalis like lightly fried fish in a sauce Westerners would regard as curry-flavoured, yet it is relatively mild. Bengalis also love sweet dishes.

## South India

In the south of India one finds a Brahmin cuisine, which is distinct because strict South Indian Brahmins will not eat tomatoes, beetroot, garlic or onions. Recipes are based on tamarind, chilli, coconut, yellow lentils and rice. These, combined with a vegetable, make sambar, a staple dish eaten with rasam, a peppery, lentil-based consommé. These two dishes are the basis of the English-inspired mulligatawny. Meat and seafood are enjoyed by non-vegetarians. Steamed dumplings and pancakes made from fermented ground rice and dhal have spread from Southern India throughout India.

## Goa

The Christian Portuguese had a great deal of influence on the tropical state of Goa, as did the Muslims. The Portuguese use of vinegar and the sour candied fruits of lokum and tamarind have combined with the Christian preference for pork and a non-vegetarian Hindu taste for lamb. Seafood, fish and fruits are plentiful. Goans also perfected the vindaloo. Try the pork vindaloo recipe on page 153, or for something milder, the cashew nut butter chicken on page 113.

# Spices, mixes & blends

# Green masala curry paste

**Makes about 1 cup/8 fl oz/250 ml**

*1 tsp fenugreek seeds, soaked in cold water overnight*
*3 cloves garlic, crushed*
*2 tbsp fresh ginger, grated (shredded)*
*scant 1 cup/240 ml fresh coriander (cilantro), chopped*
*scant 1 cup/240 ml fresh mint, chopped*
*½ cup/3½ fl oz/100 ml vinegar*
*1 tsp Thai fish sauce (nam pla)*
*2 tsp ground turmeric*
*1 tsp ground cardamom*
*¼ cup/2 fl oz/50 ml sesame oil*
*½ cup/3½ fl oz/100 ml vegetable oil*

Place soaked fenugreek seeds, garlic, ginger, coriander, mint and vinegar in a food processor or blender and process to make a smooth paste. Add fish sauce, turmeric and cardamom and process to combine.

Heat the sesame and vegetable oils together in a small pan over a medium heat for 5 minutes or until hot. Stir in paste and cook, stirring constantly, for 5 minutes or until mixture boils and thickens.

# Vindaloo curry paste

**Makes about 4 tbsp/80 ml**

*1 tbsp coriander seeds*
*1 tsp cumin seeds*
*1 tsp mustard seeds*
*1 tsp ground turmeric*
*1 tsp chilli powder*
*1½ tsp ground ginger*
*pinch of ground fenugreek*
*1½ tsp finely ground black pepper*
*1 tbsp white wine vinegar, plus extra to serve*

Using a mortar and pestle, or a coffee grinder kept especially for the purpose, finely grind the whole seeds. Add the remaining ground spices.

Gradually stir in the vinegar to make a thick, smooth paste. Store in an airtight container and moisten with an additional 1 tsp of vinegar just before use.

**Note**: Leftover paste may be stored in sterile airtight container in the refrigerator for 8–10 days.

# Tandoori spice mix

**Makes ½ cup/4 fl oz/120 ml**

*1 small onion, chopped*
*3 cloves garlic, crushed*
*1 in/2.5 cm piece fresh ginger, finely chopped*
*1–2 green chillies, seeded and chopped*
*1 tsp coriander seeds*
*½ tsp cumin seeds*
*½ tsp red chilli powder*
*1 tsp paprika*
*½ tsp salt*

Grind the onion, garlic, ginger, chillies and seeds together, using a pestle and mortar, or a coffee grinder kept especially for the purpose. Add the chilli powder, paprika and salt and mix well.

# Garam masala

**Makes 4 tbsp/80 ml**

*2 tsp cardamom seeds*
*2 tsp cumin seeds*
*2 tsp coriander seeds*
*1 tsp black peppercorns*
*1 tsp whole cloves*
*1 cinnamon stick, broken*
*½ nutmeg, grated (shredded)*

Heat a heavy frying pan over moderate heat. Add the cardamom seeds, cumin seeds, coriander seeds, peppercorns, cloves and cinnamon stick. Cook, stirring, until evenly browned. Allow to cool.

Using a mortar and pestle, or a coffee grinder kept especially for the purpose, grind the roasted spices to a fine powder. Add nutmeg and mix well.

# Aadoo mirch spice mix

**Makes 4 tbsp/80 ml**

*4 tbsp fresh ginger, grated (shredded)*
*1 clove garlic, chopped*
*12 small fresh chillies, chopped*
*½ tsp salt*

Grind ginger and garlic in a blender or food processor, or use a mortar and pestle. Add the chillies and salt. Purée to a smooth paste, scrape into a bowl and cover tightly. Will keep for 1 week in the refrigerator.

# Masala curry paste

**Makes about 1 cup/8 fl oz/ 250 ml**

*3 tbsp fresh ginger, grated (shredded)*
*1 tsp ground turmeric*
*1 tsp ground cloves*
*1 tsp ground cardamom*
*2 cloves garlic, crushed*
*½ cup/4 fl oz/120 ml fresh coriander (cilantro), chopped*
*½ cup/4 fl oz/120 ml fresh mint, chopped*
*½ cup/4 fl oz/120 ml cider vinegar*
*3 tbsp peanut oil*
*2 tsp sesame oil*

Place ginger, turmeric, cloves, cardamom, garlic, coriander, mint and vinegar in a blender or food processor; process until well combined.

Heat the oils in a frying pan. Add spice mixture. Cook, stirring, until mixture boils, then remove from heat and allow to cool.

# Madras curry paste

**Makes about ¾ cup/6 fl oz/175 ml**

½ cup/4 fl oz/ 120 ml  ground coriander
4 tbsp ground cumin
1 tbsp freshly ground black pepper
1 tbsp ground turmeric
1 tbsp black mustard seeds
1 tbsp chilli powder
4 cloves garlic, crushed
1 tbsp fresh ginger, finely grated
½ cup/4 fl oz/120 ml vinegar
2 tbsp oil

Place the coriander, cumin, black pepper, turmeric, mustard seeds, chilli powder, garlic, ginger and vinegar in a food processor or blender and process to make a smooth paste.

Heat the oil in a frying pan over medium heat, add paste and cook, stirring constantly, for 5 minutes or until oil begins to separate from paste.

# Side dishes

# Vegetable samosas

**Makes 40**

*4 sheets unsweetened short pastry*
*3 tbsp peanut oil*
*1 small onion, finely chopped*
*1 tsp curry powder*
*14 oz/400 g can potatoes, drained and quartered*
*¼ cup/1 oz/25 g frozen peas*
*¼ bunch parsley, chopped*
*1 tbsp lemon juice*

Preheat the oven to 200°C/400°F/Gas mark 6. Roll pastry out very thin. Cut five 4 in/10 cm-diameter circles from each sheet of pastry. Cut circles in half.

Heat 1 tbsp of oil in a frying pan and sauté onion for 5 minutes or until clear. Add curry powder and cook for 30 seconds or until curry smells fragrant. Mix potato, peas, onion mixture, parsley and lemon juice together.

Place a teaspoon of potato mixture on each pastry semi-circle. Wet pastry edges and fold dough over to form a cone shape. Cover with a damp kitchen towel while preparing remaining samosas.

Place on a baking sheet and bake for 15 minutes, turning after 10 minutes. Brush with remaining oil and serve immediately.

# Chickpea & eggplant dip

**Serves 4**

*2 eggplants (aubergines)*
*7 oz/200 g can chickpeas (garbanzos), drained and rinsed*
*1 cup/8 oz/225 g natural (plain) yogurt*
*juice of 1 lemon*
*1 clove garlic, crushed*
*½ cup fresh mint, chopped*
*freshly ground black pepper*
*flatbread, to serve*

Place eggplants on a baking sheet and bake for 30 minutes or until very soft. Set aside to cool, then remove skins.

Place eggplant flesh, chickpeas, yogurt, lemon juice, garlic, mint and black pepper in a food processor or blender and process until smooth. Place dip in a serving dish and serve with warm flatbread.

# Naan bread

**Serves 4**

1 cup/8 oz/225 g natural (plain) yogurt
2 cups/8 oz/225 g plain (all-purpose) flour
3 cups/12 oz/350 g stoneground
    wholemeal (wholewheat) plain
    (all-purpose) flour
1 tbsp yeast

2 tsp salt
1 tsp sugar
2 tbsp nut oil, plus extra for
    greasing bowl
3 tbsp black sesame seeds
½ cup/4 fl oz/120 ml sesame seeds

Preheat the oven to 230°C/450°F/Gas mark 8.

Mix yogurt with 1½ cups/12 fl oz/350 ml boiling water and stir well. Set aside for 5 minutes.

Mix plain flour with 1 cup/4 oz/ 115 g of wholemeal flour and add yeast. Add yogurt mixture and stir with a wooden spoon for 3 minutes, then cover with cling film (plastic wrap). Allow to rest for 1 hour.

Add salt, sugar, oil and black sesame seeds and enough of the remaining flour to form a firm but moist dough. Begin to knead on a floured surface and continue until dough is very silky and elastic. Allow dough to rise in an oiled bowl for 1 hour at room temperature or until doubled in size.

Knock back (punch down) the dough and divide into 8 pieces. Shape each into a ball then flatten each into a rough circle about ½ in/12 mm thick. Transfer to oiled baking sheets.

Brush the surface of the dough with water and sprinkle surface generously with sesame seeds.

Cover dough and allow to rise for 10 minutes. Bake for 5–8 minutes.

# Chapatis

**Makes 15**

*9 oz/250 g wholemeal (wholewheat) flour*
*1 tsp salt*

Sift flour and salt into a bowl. Make a well in the centre and add 1 cup/ 8 fl oz/250 ml of water, a little at a time, using your fingers to incorporate the surrounding flour to make a smooth, pliable dough.

Knead dough on a lightly floured surface for 5–10 minutes, then place in a bowl, cover with a cloth and leave to rest for 30–60 minutes.

Knead dough for 2–3 minutes. Divide into 6 balls of equal size, then flatten each ball a circle, about 5 in/12 cm in diameter.

Heat a dry frying pan until hot. Place one chapati at a time on the hot surface. As soon as bubbles appear on the surface of the chapati, turn the bread over. Press down on chapati with a thick cloth so that it cooks evenly.

Remove with a fish slice and hold each carefully over an open gas flame without turning until it puffs up slightly. Alternatively, place the chapati under a hot grill (broiler).

Repeat with remaining dough circles. Keep cooked chapatis hot in a covered napkin-lined basket.

# Indian fresh corn bread

**Makes 4**

*9 oz/250 g fresh corn kernels*
*½ tsp salt*
*2 tbsp ground (minced) coriander*
*1¼ cups/5 oz/145 g plain (all-purpose) flour, plus extra for dusting*
*1–2 tbsp ghee, melted*

In a blender or food processor, grind corn and salt together until it is a fine powder.

Transfer mixture to a bowl and add coriander. Add flour, a little at a time, continuing until mixture is kneadable (it should be a little tacky).

Divide dough into 12 pieces, then roll each piece into a circle about 6 in/15 cm diameter. If dough circles are too tacky, use extra flour to absorb dough moisture. Once rolled, brush each with a little ghee.

Heat a griddle or frying pan and add a little ghee. Add one piece of dough and cook until dough underside is spotted with brown. Turn and cook other side. Remove cooked bread and keep warm in foil while cooking other breads the same way.

**Note**: While many Westerners are unfamiliar with the breads of India, there are dozens of delicious and flavoursome varieties. This unusual yeast-free bread is from the area of Rajasthan in the west of the country.

If you would like to duplicate the smoky roasted flavour that these breads would have when cooked over an open fire, simply hold each bread over a gas flame for a few seconds. Do not allow to burn. Brush with more ghee and serve.

# Coconut poori

**Makes 14**

*1 cup/4 oz/115 g wholemeal (wholewheat) flour (or Indian atta flour)*
*½ cup/2 oz/55 g plain (all-purpose) flour*
*½–1 tsp salt*
*3½ oz/100 g desiccated (dry, shredded unsweetened) coconut*
*1 tsp chilli powder*
*½ tbsp sugar*
*2 tbsp ghee or vegetable oil*

Mix wholemeal flour, plain flour, salt and coconut in a bowl with chilli powder and sugar. Add melted ghee or oil and rub through until flour appears crumbly. Stir in about ½ cup/4 fl oz/120 ml water (adding only as much as necessary to form a soft dough). Knead dough well. Allow the dough to rest for 10 minutes.

Divide the dough into 14 pieces, flattening and rolling each to a thin circle of 8 cm/3 in diameter.

Heat oil in a wok and, when hot, add one circle of dough. With a heatproof implement, push dough under oil until dough is puffed and golden. Allow it to float, turning to cook the other side.

Drain on absorbent paper and cook remaining poori the same way.

**Note**: Poori are one of the most popular breads in India. These puffed-up pillow-style breads are fun to make and taste delicious.

# Indian pancakes

**Makes 25**

*1½ cups/6 oz/175 g rice flour*
*1 tsp salt*
*½ tsp baking powder*
*3 spring onions (scallions), trimmed and finely chopped*
*14 oz/400 g can coconut milk*
*2 eggs, lightly beaten*
*olive oil*

Mix the rice flour, salt, baking powder and spring onions together. Add half the coconut milk, eggs and whisk until smooth. Whisk in remaining coconut milk.

Grease a small frying pan with oil. Spoon about 2 tbsp of batter into pan. Cook over a medium heat until lightly brown. Turn and cook the other side. Keep warm and serve with curries.

# Moong sprouts

**Serves 4**

1 cup/250 ml moong sprouts,
  ¼ in/5 mm long
1 large onion, chopped
1 tsp salt
½ tsp turmeric
1 tsp green masala
½ tsp fresh ginger, pounded
½ tsp fresh garlic, pounded
2 tsp coriander-cumin

VAGAAR
½ cup/4 fl oz/120 ml cooking oil
1 dried red chilli
5 ml/1 tsp cumin seeds

GARNISH
1 tbsp coriander leaves, chopped

In a large bowl, mix together the moong sprouts, the onion, salt, turmeric, green masala, ginger, garlic and coriander-cumin.

To make the vagaar, heat the oil in a small pan with a well-fitting lid. Brown the chilli, followed by the cumin seeds. Add the sprout mixture to the pan with the warm water. Cover the pot and cook over a medium heat for about 45 minutes. (The sprouts should be soft but not stick together.) Garnish with the coriander leaves.

**Time**: 1 hour, 1–2 days for sprouting

# Bombay hot lentils

**Serves 4**

7 oz/200 g mung dhal (small yellow
   lentils), cleaned and soaked
½ tsp ground turmeric
1 in/2.5 cm piece fresh ginger,
   finely chopped
1 tbsp vegetable oil
salt and freshly ground black pepper
1 tbsp tamarind
1 tbsp brown sugar
½ bunch fresh coriander (cilantro), leaves
   removed and chopped
3 tbsp flaked coconut

2 tsp garam masala

WHOLE SPICE MIXTURE
3 oz/85 g ghee or butter
1 tsp cumin seeds
1 tsp black mustard seeds
¼ tsp fenugreek seeds
2 tbsp chopped curry leaves
3 fresh red or green chillies, finely chopped
2 in/5 cm piece fresh ginger, finely chopped
salt

Place 2 cups/475 ml/16 fl oz water in a large pan and bring to the boil. Stir in lentils, turmeric, ginger, oil, salt and pepper to taste and cook over a low heat, stirring occasionally for 30–45 minutes or until lentils are very soft. Remove pan from heat and mash lentil mixture.

Place tamarind in a small bowl, pour over 1 cup/8 fl oz/250 ml hot water and set aside to soak for 20 minutes. Drain liquid from tamarind mixture, then push tamarind pulp through a fine sieve (strainer) and set aside. Reserve juice for another use.

For spice mixture, heat ghee or butter in a large pan, add remaining ingredients and cook, stirring for 1 minute.

Add lentil mixture and 4 cups/1¾ pints/1 litre water to spice mixture and bring to the boil. Stir tamarind pulp and brown sugar into lentil mixture and cook, stirring occasionally for 5 minutes longer.

Stir in coriander, coconut and garam masala and cook for 2 minutes longer.

# Spicy yogurt rice

**Serves 4**

1 cup/7 oz/200 g long grain rice
1 cup/8 oz/225 g natural (plain) yogurt
1 tsp salt
2 green chillies, deseeded and thinly sliced
3 in/8 cm piece fresh ginger, grated (shredded)
1 tbsp peanut oil
1 tbsp black mustard seeds
¼ cup fresh coriander (cilantro), chopped

Combine the rice with 1½ cups/12 fl oz/350 ml water in a large pan. Bring to the boil, reduce heat to low, cover and cook for 15 minutes. Remove pan from heat, allow to stand covered for 10 minutes. Mix in yogurt and salt while rice is hot.

Mix chillies and ginger through rice mixture.

Heat oil in a frying pan and carefully pop mustard seeds over a low heat. Add to rice with coriander. Mix until combined, then serve.

**Note**: This is a traditional Southern Indian rice dish served at room temperature as a curry accompaniment.

# Lentil & rice dumplings

**Serves 8**

1½ cups/6 oz/175 g white urad dhal flour
½ cup/2 oz/55 g rice flour
4 fresh green chillies, finely chopped
2.5 cm/1 in piece ginger, finely chopped
¼ tsp bicarbonate of soda
  (baking soda)
2 tsp sultanas (golden raisins)
2 tsp salted cashews, chopped
2 tsp blanched almonds, chopped
salt and freshly ground black pepper

1 bunch fresh coriander (cilantro), leaves
  removed and chopped
vegetable oil, for deep-frying
1 cup /225 g/8 oz natural (plain) yogurt
¼ tsp mango powder
¼ tsp ground cumin
¼ tsp ground coriander
¼ tsp paprika
¼ tsp black salt
1 tbsp black mustard seeds
5–7 fresh or dried curry leaves

Place flours, chillies, ginger, bicarbonate of soda, sultanas, cashews, almonds, seasoning and half the coriander in a bowl. Stir in enough water to make a thick, smooth batter, mix well, cover and set aside for 1 hour.

Heat oil in a wok. Gently pat a spoonful of batter in the palm of your hand to form a dumpling. Cook 4–5 dumplings at a time in hot oil until golden. Using a slotted spoon remove dumplings from oil and drop into a bowl of warm water. Allow to soak for 5–7 minutes, then remove and squeeze between the palms of your hands to flatten and remove excess water. Arrange on a flat serving dish.

Beat yogurt and ¼ cup/2 fl oz/50 ml water in a bowl until smooth. Spoon a over the dumplings.

Mix mango powder, cumin, ground coriander, paprika and salt. Set aside.

Heat 2 tbsp of hot oil from wok, in a metal ladle over low heat. Add mustard seeds and curry leaves and heat until they sizzle. Pour over dumplings, sprinkle with spice mixture and remaining fresh coriander. Serve.

# Roasted red capsicum raita

**Serves 4**

*2 red capsicums (bell peppers)*
*2 tsp cumin seeds*
*scant 1 cup/7 oz/200 g Greek (strained plain) yogurt*
*2 tbsp fresh mint, finely chopped*
*salt and freshly ground black pepper*
*1 tsp paprika, to garnish*

Heat the grill (broiler) to high. Cut the capsicums lengthwise into quarters, then remove the seeds and grill (broil), skin-side up, for 10 minutes or until blackened and blistered. Place in a plastic bag, seal and leave to cool for 10 minutes.

Toast the cumin seeds in a small frying pan, stirring constantly over medium to high heat, until aromatic. Remove and reserve.

Peel the skins from the grilled capsicum and discard, then roughly chop the flesh. Mix the capsicum with the yogurt, cumin seeds and mint and season to taste. Transfer to a serving dish and garnish with the paprika.

**Note**: Red capsicum adds colour as well as a slight sweetness to this cooling side dish. It can be made the day before and kept in refrigerated.

# Spicy wholemeal parathas

**Makes 12**

*3 cups/12 oz/350 g flour*
*1 cup/4 oz/115 g wholemeal (wholewheat) flour*
*4 oz/115 g butter*
*8 oz/250 g mashed potato*
*4 oz/115 g lentils, drained*
*4 oz/115 g mature (sharp) Cheddar cheese, grated (shredded)*
*2 tsp curry powder*
*1 tsp ground cumin*

Place flours in a food processor and process to sift. Add half the butter and process until mixture resembles coarse breadcrumbs.

With machine running, add 1½ cups/12 fl oz/350 ml water and process to form a dough. Turn dough onto a lightly floured surface and knead for 5 minutes or until smooth. Set aside for 5 minutes.

Place mashed potato, lentils, cheese, curry powder and cumin in a bowl and mix to combine.

Divide dough into twelve equal portions and press out each portion to form a 4 in/10 cm circle. Divide potato mixture between dough circles and spread evenly over dough, leaving a border around the edge. Fold dough circles in half to enclose the filling, then carefully roll again to form a 4 in/10 cm circle.

Melt remaining butter in a large frying pan and cook a few parathas at a time for 3–4 minutes each side, or until golden and cooked through.

# Potato naan

**Serves 4**

| | |
|---|---|
| 1 cup/8 oz/225 g natural (plain) yogurt | FILLING |
| 2 cups/8 oz/225 g plain (all-purpose) flour | 1 lb/450 g potatoes, peeled and diced |
| 3 cups/12 oz/350 g stoneground | 1 onion, finely diced |
|    wholemeal (wholewheat) flour | 4 mint leaves, finely sliced |
| 1 tbsp yeast | ¼ bunch parsley, chopped |
| 2 tsp salt | ½ bunch coriander (cilantro) leaves, |
| 1 tsp sugar |    chopped |
| 2 tbsp peanut oil | ¼ tsp ground cumin |
| 3 tbsp black sesame seeds | ¼ tsp ground turmeric |
| 1 egg, beaten | salt and freshly ground black pepper |

Preheat oven to 200°C/400°F/Gas mark 6. Mix yogurt with 1½ cups/12 fl oz/ 350 ml boiling water and stir well. Set aside for 5 minutes.

Mix the plain flour with one-third of the wholemeal flour. Add the yeast, then the yogurt mixture and stir for 3 minutes. Set aside for 30 minutes.

Add salt, sugar, oil and black sesame seeds and enough of the remaining flour to form a firm but moist dough. Knead on a floured surface until dough is elastic. Allow to rest in an oiled bowl for 1 hour or until doubled in size.

To make the potato filling, boil until soft. Drain, then mix hot potato with onion, mint leaves, parsley, coriander, cumin, turmeric and salt and pepper and mash until soft but not sloppy. Cool.

Knock back (punch down) dough and divide into 12 equal pieces. Roll each piece into a 6 in/15 cm circle. Place a large tablespoon of filling in the centre of each dough circle and lift the edges of circle to seal. Pinch seam together. Allow to rise for 10 minutes then brush with beaten egg and sprinkle with sesame seeds. Bake for 15–20 minutes or until golden and crisp.

# Fragrant pilau rice

**Serves 4**

*large pinch of saffron strands*
*8 oz/225 g basmati rice*
*1 oz/25 g butter*
*1 spring onion (scallion), finely chopped*
*3 cardamom pods*
*1 cinnamon stick*
*salt*

Briefly grind the saffron using a mortar and pestle, then mix the powder with 1 tbsp of boiling water and set aside. Rinse the rice and drain.

Melt the butter in a large, heavy pan. Fry the spring onion gently for 2 minutes or until softened. Add the cardamom pods, cinnamon and rice and mix well.

Add 1¾ cups/½ pint/ 300 ml of water, the saffron mixture and salt. Bring to the boil, then reduce the heat and cover the pan tightly. Simmer the rice for 15 minutes or until the liquid has been absorbed and the rice is tender. Remove the cardamom pods and cinnamon stick before serving.

# Spiced yogurt dip

**Serves 4**

*½ tsp cumin seeds*
*¼ tsp ground turmeric*
*11oz/300g natural (plain) yogurt*
*1 tbsp lemon juice*

Cook the spices in a small frying pan over medium heat until fragrant. Remove from the heat and leave to cool.

Place the yogurt in a small bowl. Add the spices and lemon juice and stir to combine. Transfer to a small serving dish.

# Coconut sambal

**Serves 4**

*2 oz/55 g desiccated (dry unsweetened shredded) coconut*
*1 tbsp onion, finely chopped*
*1 small red chilli, seeded and chopped*
*1 tbsp lime juice*

Mix coconut, onion and chilli in a small bowl. Add lime juice, toss lightly and serve.

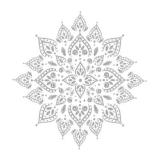

# Split lentil dhal with ginger & coriander

**Serves 4**

*7 oz/200 g dried split red lentils*
*½ tsp turmeric*
*1 tbsp vegetable oil*
*½ in/1 cm piece fresh ginger, finely chopped*
*1 tsp cumin seeds*
*1 tsp ground coriander*
*salt and freshly ground black pepper*
*⅓ cup fresh coriander (cilantro), chopped*
*½ tsp paprika*

Rinse the lentils and drain well, then place in a large pan with 3¾ cups 1½ pints/900 ml/of water. Bring to the boil, skimming any scum, then stir in the turmeric. Reduce the heat and partly cover the pan. Simmer for 30–35 minutes, stirring occasionally, until thickened.

Heat the oil in a small frying pan, then add the ginger and cumin seeds and fry for 30 seconds or until the cumin seeds start to pop. Stir in the ground coriander and cook for 1 minute.

Season the lentils with plenty of salt and pepper, then add the toasted spices. Stir in the chopped coriander, mixing well. Transfer to a serving dish and garnish with the paprika and extra coriander leaves.

**Note**: Dhal is very much an everyday dish in Indian households. Ginger and fresh coriander add extra zest to this version of the slowly simmered lentil purée.

# Vegetarian

# Bean curry

**Serves 4**

1 onion, peeled
2 in/5 cm piece fresh root ginger, peeled
2 cloves garlic, peeled
1 tbsp olive oil
2 tsp curry powder
1 tsp ground cumin
1 tsp turmeric
⅓ cup sweet fruit chutney
⅓ cup crunchy peanut butter
14 oz/400 g can peeled tomatoes
¼ cup tomato paste
14 oz/400 g can cannellini beans, drained
14 oz/400 g can borlotti beans, drained

Place roughly chopped onion, ginger and garlic in processor and blend until smooth.

Heat oil in pan, cook onion mixture, stirring occasionally for 5 minutes, add curry, cumin and turmeric and cook, stirring for 1 minute.

Add chutney, peanut butter, tomatoes, tomato paste, 1 cup/8 fl oz/250 ml of water and beans. Stir until well combined. Bring to boil, reduce heat and simmer covered 20 minutes. Serve with rice.

# Simple pilau rice

**Serves 4–6**

*14 oz/400 g basmati rice, rinsed*
*6 cloves*
*2 in/5 cm piece cinnamon stick, crushed*
*6 green cardamom pods, crushed*
*½ tsp ground turmeric*
*2 oz/55 g raisins*
*1 oz/30 g slivered (flaked) almonds*
*2 bay leaves*
*1 tbsp sugar*
*salt*
*⅔ cup/¼ pint/140 ml melted ghee or oil*
*½ tsp cumin seeds*
*1 tbsp fresh root ginger, grated (shredded)*

Soak rice in cold water for 10 minutes. Drain and spread out on a clean cloth to dry.

Transfer rice to a platter. Sprinkle over whole cloves, a few pieces of cinnamon stick, the cardamom pods, turmeric, raisins, almonds, bay leaves, sugar and salt.

Drizzle over ½ tsp of melted ghee or oil. Using your hand, mix spices thoroughly into rice. Leave for 15 minutes.

Heat remaining ghee or oil in a large pan. Add cumin seeds, ginger and rice mixture. Fry gently for 5 minutes until rice is transparent.

Add hot water to cover rice by ½ in/1 cm. Bring to the boil, lower heat and simmer until all liquid is absorbed and rice is tender. Before serving, turn rice over gently.

# South Indian spiced rice with green beans & peas

**Serves 4**

2 cups/14 oz/400 g basmati rice
3½ oz/100 g peas
3½ oz/100 g green beans, chopped

BHATH MASALA
1¾ oz/50 g channa dhal
3 oz/75 g urad dhal

4 red dried chillies
8 whole cloves
2 cardamom pods
1 cinnamon stick
3 tbsp desiccated (dry, unsweetened
  shredded) coconut
3 tbsp coriander seeds

To make the bhath masala, dry roast the channa dhal. Add the rest of bhath masala ingredients. Dry roast until you smell a toasted aroma. The lentils should then be roasted nicely.

Place into a mortar and pestle and grind coarsely.

Put the rice into a pan, add 2½ cups/18 fl oz/ 550 ml water and bring to the boil. Place a lid on the pan and reduce the heat to a low setting.

Gently simmer for 15 minutes, then turn off heat and let it steam for another 10 minutes.

Blanch the peas and beans.

Transfer the rice into a large bowl and fluff with fork. Add 4 tbsp of bhath masala, mix well, and add the beans and peas.

Serve warm. More bhath masala may be added, if desired.

# Vegetable & lentil curry

**Serves 4**

1 tbsp olive oil
1 onion, sliced
1 clove garlic, crushed
1 tsp ground cumin
1 tsp ground coriander
1 tsp ground turmeric
2 carrots, sliced
3½ oz/100 g red lentils
7 oz/200 g can tomatoes, mashed with
   the juice

1½ cups/12 fl oz/ 350 ml vegetable stock
   or water
1 tsp chilli sauce
1 lb/450 g pumpkin or potatoes, cut into
   1 in/2.5 cm cubes
½ cauliflower, cut into florets
2 tbsp blanched almonds
freshly ground black pepper
4 tbsp natural yogurt

Heat oil in a large pan, add onion, garlic, cumin, coriander, turmeric and carrots and cook for 5 minutes or until onion is soft.

Stir in lentils, tomatoes and stock or water and bring to the boil. Reduce heat, cover and simmer for 15 minutes.

Add chilli sauce, pumpkin or potatoes and cauliflower and cook for 15–20 minutes longer or until pumpkin or potatoes are tender. Stir in almonds and black pepper to taste. To serve, ladle curry into bowls and top with a spoonful of yogurt.

# Moghul salad

**Serves 6**

*7 oz/200 g mung bean sprouts*
*3 cucumbers, diced*
*1 tbsp grated (shredded) fresh or desiccated (dry, unsweetened shredded) coconut*
*2 tomatoes, diced*
*¼ bunch fresh coriander (cilantro) leaves, chopped*
*½ bunch fresh mint leaves, chopped*
*½ bunch fresh basil leaves, chopped*
*1 bunch spring onions (scallions), chopped*
*2 tbsp lemon juice*
*salt and freshly ground black pepper*

Place bean sprouts, cucumbers, coconut, tomatoes, coriander, mint and basil leaves, spring onions, lemon juice, and salt and black pepper in a bowl and toss to combine. Cover and stand at room temperature for 2–3 hours before serving.

# Fresh mint chutney

**Makes 2 cups**

*4 spring onions (scallions)*
*2 fresh green chillies*
*1 cup firmly packed fresh mint leaves*
*¼ tsp salt*
*1 tsp sugar*
*1 tsp garam masala*
*¼ cup/2 fl oz/50 ml lime juice*

Trim spring onions and chop roughly. Deseed chillies and chop roughly. Place spring onions, chillies, mint leaves, salt, sugar, garam masala and lime juice in a food processor or blender. Process until smooth. Serve as an accompaniment to curries or roast lamb.

**Note**: For a different flavour, add 40–60 ml/2–3 tablespoons of natural (plain) yogurt to this.

# Indian spiced potato & onion soup

**Serves 4**

1 tbsp vegetable oil
1 onion, finely chopped
½ in/1 cm piece root ginger, finely chopped
2 large potatoes, cut into ½ in/1 cm cubes
2 tsp ground cumin
2 tsp ground coriander
½ tsp turmeric
1 tsp ground cinnamon
4 cups/1¾ pints/1 litre vegetable stock
salt and freshly ground black pepper
1 tbsp natural (plain) yogurt, to garnish

Heat the oil in a large pan. Fry the onion and ginger for 5 minutes or until softened. Add the potatoes and sauté for another minute, stirring often.

Mix the cumin, coriander, turmeric and cinnamon with 2 tbsp of cold water to make a paste. Add to the onion and potato, stirring well, and fry for 1 minute or until aromatic.

Add the stock and season to taste. Bring to the boil, then reduce the heat, cover and simmer for 30 minutes or until the potato is tender. Blend until smooth in a food processor, or press through a metal sieve (strainer). Return to the pan and gently heat through. Garnish with the yogurt and more black pepper.

**Note**: This delicately spiced soup makes a great start to an Indian meal. But it can also make a satisfying snack on its own if you serve it with warm naan bread and a salad.

# Chickpea salad with spinach

**Serves 4**

2 cups/14 oz/400 g dried chickpeas
  (garbanzos)
4 onions
1 tsp whole cloves
4 bay leaves
¼ cup/2 fl oz/50 ml peanut or olive oil
4 cloves garlic, crushed
1 tsp turmeric

2 tsp cumin
2 tsp garam masala
2 tbsp tomato paste
2 red capsicums (bell peppers), sliced
4 medium zucchini (courgettes), sliced on
  the diagonal
salt and pepper to taste
1¼ lb/500 g baby spinach

Pick over the chickpeas and remove any that are discoloured. Place all remaining chickpeas in a large pan and cover with cold water.

Peel 2 of the onions and chop in half. Place these in the pan with the chickpeas. Add the cloves and bay leaves and bring to the boil and simmer for 10 minutes then remove from the heat and cover and allow to steep for 2 hours. Strain the chickpeas, discarding the onions, cloves and bay leaves, and reserving 2 cups/16 fl oz/475 ml of the soaking water.

Chop the remaining 2 onions. Heat the oil and sauté the onions and the garlic. Add all the spices and cook briefly to release their fragrance. Add the soaked chickpeas and 2 cups of the soaking water, the tomato paste and the capsicum slices.

Cover and simmer gently for about 20 minutes until the chickpeas soften and the liquid evaporates. Add the zucchini and salt and pepper to taste and stir well then remove from the heat. Allow to cool slightly then fold through the spinach leaves. Cool completely and serve.

# Red lentils

**Serves 6**

1½ cups red lentils, cleaned and soaked
1 tsp vegetable oil
½ in/12 mm piece fresh ginger,
  finely chopped
¼ tsp ground turmeric
salt and freshly ground black pepper

*TOMATO AND ONION SAUCE*
2 tbsp vegetable oil
1 in/2.5 cm piece fresh ginger,
  finely chopped
2 fresh red or green chillies, chopped

3 onions, chopped
4 tomatoes, diced
2 tbsp ghee or butter
¼ tsp cumin seeds
¼ tsp fennel seeds
¼ tsp black mustard seeds
¼ tsp fenugreek seeds
¼ tsp black onion seeds
3 dried red chillies
2 bay leaves
2 tsp garlic paste

Place 2 cups/16 fl oz/475 ml water in a pan and bring to the boil. Add lentils, 1 tsp oil, ginger, turmeric and salt to taste and cook, partially covered, for 10–15 minutes or until lentils are soft and pulpy.

To make sauce, heat oil in a heavy pan, add ginger, chillies and onions, cover and cook over a medium heat for 10–15 minutes or until onions are golden.

Stir in tomatoes and cook over a low heat for 10–15 minutes or until tomatoes are soft. Stir lentil mixture and 4 cups water into tomato mixture and bring to the boil.

Heat ghee or butter in a frying pan, add cumin seeds, fennel seeds, mustard seeds, fenugreek seeds, black onion seeds, ginger, bay leaves and garlic paste and cook for 2 minutes.

Stir spice mixture into boiling lentil mixture, cover and cook for 2 minutes longer.

# Thoor lentils

**Serves 8**

*3 cups thoor dhal (medium flat yellow lentils), cleaned and soaked*
*2 tbsp vegetable oil*
*1 tsp cumin seeds*
*1 tsp yellow mustard seeds*
*5 curry leaves*
*1 tsp fenugreek seeds*
*1 in/2.5 cm piece fresh ginger, chopped*
*2 fresh red or green chillies, finely chopped*
*salt and freshly ground black pepper*
*1 cup coriander (cilantro), chopped*

Place 1¾ pints/4 cups/1 litre water in a large saucepan and bring to the boil. Stir in lentils and 1 tablespoon oil, reduce heat to low and simmer, stirring frequently and removing froth. Cook for 10–15 minutes or until lentils are soft and pulpy.

Heat the remaining oil in a heavy pan and add cumin seeds, curry leaves, yellow mustard seeds, fenugreek seeds, ginger and chillies. Cook over a low heat for 2–3 minutes, until spices are fragrant and start to pop, stir in cooked lentils.

Remove pan from heat, season lentil mixture to taste with salt and sprinkle with fresh coriander.

# Vegetable korma

**Serves 4**

2 tbsp vegetable oil
2 tbsp green masala curry paste
1 tsp chilli powder
1 tbsp fresh ginger, finely grated (shredded)
2 cloves garlic, crushed
1 onion, chopped
1¼ lb/500 g cauliflower, cut into florets
7 oz/200 g green beans
3 baby eggplants (aubergines)
2 carrots, sliced
4½ oz/125 g button (white) mushrooms
14 oz /400 g can tomatoes, mashed in their juices
250 ml/8 fl oz/1 cup vegetable stock

Heat oil in a pan over medium heat, stir in masala paste and chilli powder and cook for 2 minutes. Add ginger, garlic and onion and cook, stirring, for 3 minutes or until onion is soft. Add cauliflower, beans, eggplants, carrots and mushrooms and cook, stirring, for 5 minutes.

Stir in tomatoes and stock, and bring to the boil. Reduce heat and simmer, stirring occasionally, for 20 minutes or until vegetables are tender.

# Potato & pea bhajis

**Serves 4**

*3–4 tbsp oil*
*1 onion, thinly sliced*
*1 tsp ground turmeric*
*1 tsp cumin seeds*
*¼ tsp ground ginger*
*1 green chilli, seeded and chopped*
*1¼ lb/500 g potatoes, peeled and diced*
*9 oz/250 g fresh or frozen peas (thawed if frozen)*
*fresh coriander (cilantro) leaves, chopped, to garnish*

Heat oil in a flameproof casserole, add onion and fry for 5–7 minutes, stirring frequently, until browned but not crisp.

Stir in turmeric, cumin seeds, ginger and chilli, then add potatoes and cook gently for 5 minutes, stirring frequently.

Stir in peas. Cover casserole and simmer over very low heat for 15–20 minutes or until potatoes are tender but retain their shape. Garnish with coriander and serve.

# Lentil burger

**Serves 4**

3 oz/90 g red lentils, cooked, drained
   and mashed
8 oz/250 g potatoes, peeled and mashed
2 tbsp butter
¾ cup/6 fl oz/175 ml milk
1 egg, lightly beaten
4 spring onions (scallions), chopped
1 clove garlic, crushed
1 tsp ground cumin

1 tbsp fresh coriander (cilantro), chopped
1 tsp curry powder
freshly ground black pepper
4 bread rolls, split and toasted

YOGURT MINT SAUCE
1 cup/8 oz/ 225 g natural (plain) yogurt
1 tbsp fresh mint, chopped

To make sauce, place yogurt and mint in a small bowl and mix to combine.

Put red lentils in a pan, cover with cold water and bring to the boil. Cook for 15–20 minutes, or until the lentils are soft. Drain the lentils and mash.

Place potatoes in a large pan, cover with cold water and bring to the boil. Simmer uncovered for 20–30 minutes or until potatoes are soft to the centre. Drain the potatoes and return to the pan over low heat, allowing the potatoes to steam for a few minutes. Add milk and butter and mash until creamy.

Place lentils, mashed potato, milk, egg, spring onions, garlic, cumin, coriander, curry powder and black pepper to taste in a bowl and mix to combine.

Shape lentil mixture into eight patties and cook under a preheated grill (broiler) for 5 minutes each side or until golden and heated through.

Place a warm burger between the pieces of each toasted roll, add sauce and serve.

# Vegetable curry

**Serves 4–6**

2 tbsp vegetable oil
2½ lb/1 kg leeks, thinly sliced and washed
1¼ lb/500 g baby carrots, scrubbed and sliced diagonally
4 stalks celery, finely chopped
½ clove garlic, crushed
1 tbsp curry powder
¾ cup/6 fl oz/175 ml vegetable stock
2 tsp cornflour (cornstarch)
salt and freshly ground black pepper
6 spring onions (scallions), sliced diagonally
Rice, to serve

Heat the oil in a frying pan and lightly sauté the leeks, carrots and celery. Spoon vegetables into slow cooker. Add garlic and curry powder to frying pan and cook for 1–2 minutes.

Blend stock with cornflour (cornstarch), add to frying pan and bring to the boil, stirring constantly. Pour mixture into slow cooker and season. Cook on low for approximately 4 hours or on high for approximately 2–3 hours (test for tenderness after this, as cooking time can very greatly according to the tenderness of the vegetables).

When vegetables are cooked, add spring onions. Serve with rice.

# Root vegetable curry

**Serves 4**

1 tbsp olive oil
1 onion, chopped
1 green chilli, deseeded and chopped
1 clove garlic, finely chopped
1 in/2.5 cm piece fresh root ginger, grated
   (shredded)
2 tbsp plain (all-purpose) flour
2 tsp ground coriander
2 tsp ground cumin
2 tsp ground turmeric

1 cup/8 fl oz/250 ml vegetable stock
1 cup/8 fl oz/250 ml tomato purée (paste)
1½ lb/675 g mixed root vegetables, such
   as potato, sweet potato, celeriac and
   swede (rutabaga), diced
2 carrots, thinly sliced
freshly ground black pepper
couscous, to serve
coriander (cilantro), to garnish

Heat the oil in a large pan. Add the onion, chilli, garlic and ginger and cook, stirring occasionally, for 3 minutes. Stir in the flour, coriander, cumin and turmeric and cook gently, stirring, for 2 minutes to release the flavours.

Transfer mixture to a slow cooker and stir in the stock, then add the tomato purée, diced root vegetables and carrots. Season with pepper and mix well. Cook on high for 3¼ hours or until the vegetables are tender. Serve with steamed couscous and garnish with coriander.

# Okra & chickpea salad

**Serves 4**

6 oz/180 g dried chickpeas (garbanzos)
1½ tbsp olive oil
1 medium red onion, cut into 8 wedges
1 clove garlic, crushed
12 oz/300 g pickled okra, drained
3 tomatoes, skinned and quartered

4 tbsp chopped fresh coriander (cilantro)
1½ tbsp lemon juice
freshly ground black pepper
½ cup fresh mint leaves

Place chickpeas in a bowl, cover with cold water and set aside to soak overnight.

Drain and place in a large pan with enough cold water to cover chickpeas by 2 in/5 cm. Bring to the boil and boil rapidly for 5 minutes, then reduce heat and simmer for 1½ hours or until chickpeas are tender. Drain, and reserve 4 tbsp of cooking liquid.

Heat the oil in a large frying pan and cook onion over a low heat for 10 minutes or until golden. Add garlic, okra, chickpeas and reserved cooking liquid and cook for 4–5 minutes or until okra is tender.

Add tomatoes, coriander, lemon juice and black pepper to taste, add mint and toss to combine. Serve hot or cold.

**Note**: Okra, also known as gumbo and lady's fingers, is a close relative of the ornamental hibiscus. When buying okra, choose crisp, young, small pods. When cooked, okra should be soft but still have just a little of its crunch.

# Indian lentil soup

**Serves 4**

2 tbsp ghee or vegetable oil
13 oz/350 g red lentils
1 tsp mustard seeds
1 tsp ground coriander
1 tsp ground cumin
1½ tsp turmeric
1 cinnamon stick
6 cloves garlic, crushed
1 tbsp root ginger, minced
10 fresh curry leaves, bruised and
    tied together

1 large onion, finely chopped
1 large green chilli, whole but split
8 cups/3½ pints/2 l rich vegetable stock
2 tomatoes, finely diced
1 small eggplant (aubergine), finely diced
1 small carrot, finely diced
1 large potato, peeled and diced
juice of 4 lemons
salt, to taste
1 bunch fresh coriander (cilantro)
4 tbsp natural (plain) yogurt

In a large pan, heat ghee and add lentils, mustard seeds, ground coriander, cumin, turmeric, cinnamon, garlic, ginger, curry leaves, onion and green chilli. Cook over low heat for 5 minutes until spices are aromatic and deep brown in colour and the onion has softened.

Add vegetable stock and simmer until lentils are soft; about 30–45 minutes.

Remove cinnamon stick, whole green chilli and curry leaves.

Blend with a hand-held mixer or food processor until smooth, then return it to the pan.

Add diced vegetables and simmer for another 20 minutes or until vegetables are soft.

Add lemon juice, salt and chopped coriander. Stir well and serve with a dollop of yogurt, garnished with a few extra coriander leaves.

# Indian curried vegetable soup

**Serves 4**

2 tbsp butter or ghee
2 tsp turmeric
4 cloves garlic, ground
1 tbsp mild curry powder
1 tbsp garam masala
1 tbsp ground ginger
1 tsp chilli flakes
4 medium potatoes
2 sweet potatoes (kumera)
2 turnips
1 parsnip

4 medium carrots
1 medium butternut pumpkin
4 medium zucchini (courgettes)
14 oz/400 g peas, shelled
4 cups/1 ¾ pints/1 l vegetable stock
4 fl oz/400 ml coconut milk
salt and pepper
1 cup coriander (cilantro) leaves,
   to garnish
Toasted Indian bread, to serve
Cucumber yogurt, to serve

Heat the butter or ghee and add the turmeric, garlic, curry powder, garam masala, ginger and chilli flakes and sauté until the spices are fragrant.

Meanwhile, peel and chop all the root vegetables and the pumpkin. Slice the zucchini and shell the peas.

Add the chopped vegetables (not the zucchini and peas) to the spice mixture, add the stock and bring the soup to the boil. Simmer for 45 minutes until the vegetables are very soft.

Add the coconut milk, zucchini and peas and continue to simmer for 15 minutes. Season with salt and pepper and serve, garnished with coriander and accompanied by toasted Indian bread and cucumber yogurt.

# Curried potato & egg salad

**Serves 4**

*1 ¾ lb/800 g potatoes*
*4 hard boiled eggs*
*¼ cup chopped chives*
*2 sticks celery*
*½ cup mayonnaise*
*3 tsp curry powder*
*1 tbsp coriander (cilantro), finely chopped*

Peel potatoes and cut into cubes, then place in salted, boiling water. Cook until just tender. Drain well and place in a bowl.

Shell the eggs and chop roughly. Add to the potatoes and chives. Wash and trim celery, cut into thin slices and add to the potatoes.

Mix the mayonnaise and curry powder together and carefully mix through the potato mixture, taking care not to break up the potatoes. Serve garnished with chopped coriander.

# Cool cumin-scented yogurt soup

**Serves 6**

1 tsp cumin seeds
1 tsp nigella (black onion) seeds, plus extra
  for garnishing
1 tbsp ghee or butter
4 spring onions (scallions), finely sliced
10 fresh mint leaves
2 tsp ground cumin
1 tsp turmeric
2½ oz/60 g cashew nuts

11 oz/300 g chickpeas (garbanzos),
  drained and rinsed
1¼ lb/500 g natural (plain) yogurt
scant 1 cup/7 fl oz/200 ml sour cream
salt and pepper, to taste
1 lb 6 oz/600 g cucumbers
1 tbsp sugar
2 tbsp shredded coconut, toasted
mint leaves, for garnish

Heat a frying pan then add the cumin seeds and nigella seeds and toss around the hot pan until they smell roasted and seem to 'pop', about 3 minutes. Remove the seeds and set them aside.

Add the ghee or butter to the pan, then the spring onions and mint leaves and sauté for a few minutes until wilted. Add the cumin, turmeric and cashew nuts and toss until the spices are fragrant and the nuts are golden. Add the drained chickpeas and cook for another 2 minutes. Set aside.

In a mixing bowl, whisk together the yogurt, sour cream and scant 1 cup/ 7 fl oz/ 200 ml water until smooth. Season to taste.

Peel the cucumbers and scrape out the seeds. Cut the cucumber flesh into thin slices and add to the yogurt mixture.

Add the spring onion/spice mixture and sugar to the yogurt and stir thoroughly to combine. Allow the flavours to blend for 1 hour. Serve garnished with toasted coconut, sliced mint leaves and a few nigella seeds.

# Poultry

# Indian chicken with spiced yellow rice

**Serves 4**

1 lb 13 oz/750 g chicken wings or pieces,
   cut into bite-size pieces
½ oz/15 g butter
2 onions, thinly sliced
1 clove garlic, crushed
3 tsp curry powder
1 tsp ground ginger
½ tsp ground cinnamon
zest (shredded) and juice of 1 orange
2 cups/16 fl oz/475 ml chicken stock
2 tsp lemon juice
2 oranges, segmented
½ cup/4 oz/115 g sultanas (golden
   raisins)

3 tsp cornflour (cornstarch)
salt and freshly ground black pepper
½ cup/2 oz/55 g toasted almonds

SPICED YELLOW RICE
2 cups/14 oz/ 400 g medium-grain rice
4 cups/1¾ pints/1 l chicken stock
4 cloves
1 bay leaf
2 in/5 cm stick cinnamon
2 cardamom pods
½ tsp turmeric
salt and freshly ground black pepper
½ oz/15 g butter

Dry fry the chicken and set aside. In another pan, heat the butter in a frying pan and fry the onions and garlic until tender. Blend in curry powder, ginger and cinnamon, cook, stirring, for 1 minute.

Add the zest, juice, stock and lemon juice with orange segments and sultanas. Dissolve the cornflour in a little water and add, stir until it boils and thickens. Season with salt and pepper. Add chicken and simmer on low heat for about 5 minutes.

To make the spiced yellow rice, combine rice, stock and spices in a pan. Bring to the boil, reduce heat to low, cover and cook for 15 minutes. Season and remove pan from heat. Allow to stand covered for 10 minutes. Gently fork butter through rice before serving.

Serve the chicken with spiced yellow rice and toasted almonds.

# Chicken tropicana

**Serves 4**

*3 lb/1.3 kg roasting chicken*
*1 onion, chopped*
*1 carrot, chopped*
*1 stalk celery, chopped*
*salt and peppercorns*
*1 oz/30 g butter*
*1 tbsp plain (all-purpose) flour*
*1 tbsp curry powder*
*1 cup/8 fl oz/250 ml milk*
*juice and zest of ½ lemon*
*3 tbsp single (light) cream*
*2 large mangoes, diced*
*Coriander (cilantro), to garnish*

Place chicken in slow cooker with onion, carrot, celery, salt and peppercorns, and cover with water. Cook on low for approximately 8 hours or overnight.

Remove chicken and chop coarsely, discarding skin and bones. Retain stock for soups.

Melt the butter in a frying pan over low heat, then add the flour and curry powder and stir for 1–2 minutes. Add the milk and bring to the boil, stirring constantly, then reduce heat and simmer until thickened, stirring constantly. Season to taste, add lemon juice and zest and stir in cream.

Fold chicken and mango into sauce and pour back into slow cooker on high heat and allow to heat through. Serve with rice garnished with coriander.

# Roasted Patiala chicken breasts

**Serves 4**

*1 medium onion, peeled and puréed*
*1 tsp salt*
*4 cloves garlic, chopped*
*2 tbsp coriander (cilantro), chopped, plus extra to garnish*
*4 cardamom pods, husks discarded*
*2 tbsp natural (plain) yogurt*
*½ cup/4 oz/115 g butter, melted*
*2 tbsp tandoori spice mix*
*4 skinless chicken breasts*
*Basmati rice, to serve*

Cook the onion in a small pan over a medium heat for 5 minutes and leave to cool.

Using a mortar and pestle, grind the salt, garlic, coriander and cardamom seeds to a paste. Transfer to a non-metallic bowl, stir in the yogurt, butter, tandoori spice mix and cooked onion, and mix together well.

Score each chicken breast 4 times with a sharp knife, and coat chicken thoroughly. Cover and chill for 6 hours.

Preheat the oven to 220°C/425°F/gas mark 7. Place the chicken breasts on a rack in a roasting dish and cook for 20–25 minutes until tender and the juices run clear when the chicken is pierced with a skewer. Serve with basmati rice.

# Tikka skewers

**Serves 4**

1¼ lb/500 g chicken tenderloins
oil, for cooking
1 lemon, cut into wedges

*SPICY YOGURT MARINADE*
1 small onion, chopped
3 cloves garlic, crushed
½ in/1 cm piece fresh root ginger, finely
   grated (shredded)
1 tbsp ground cumin
1 tbsp garam masala
2 cardamom pods, crushed

1 tsp ground turmeric
1 tsp chilli powder
1 tsp ground coriander
1 tbsp tomato purée
1¼ cups/10 oz/275 g natural (plain)
   yogurt

*CUCUMBER RAITA*
1 cucumber, finely chopped
¼ cup fresh mint, chopped
1 cup/8 oz/225 g natural (plain) yogurt
Lemon wedges, to serve

Pierce tenderloins several times with a fork and place in a shallow ceramic or glass dish.

To make marinade, place onion, garlic, ginger, cumin, garam masala, cardamom, turmeric, chilli powder, coriander and tomato purée in a food processor or blender and process until smooth. Add yogurt and mix to combine. Spoon marinade over chicken, toss to combine, cover and marinate in the refrigerator for 3 hours.

Preheat barbecue to a medium heat. Drain chicken and thread onto lightly oiled skewers. Place skewers on lightly oiled barbecue rack and cook, turning several times, for 5–6 minutes or until cooked.

To make raita, place cucumber, mint and yogurt in a bowl and mix to combine. Serve skewers with lemon wedges and raita.

# Chicken rogan josh

**Serves 4**

8 skinless chicken thighs
1 tbsp vegetable oil
1 small red capsicum (bell pepper),
    thinly sliced
1 small green capsicum (bell pepper),
    thinly sliced
1 onion, thinly sliced
2 in/5 cm piece fresh root ginger,
    finely chopped
2 cloves garlic, crushed
2 tbsp garam masala

1 tsp paprika
1 tsp turmeric
1 tsp chilli powder
4 cardamom pods, crushed
salt
7 oz/200 g Greek (strained plain) yogurt
14 oz/400 g can chopped tomatoes
fresh coriander (cilantro), to garnish
Rice, mango chutney and mint raita,
    to serve

Cut each chicken thigh into 4 pieces. Heat the oil in a large, heavy frying pan and add the capsicum, onion, ginger, garlic, spices and a good pinch of salt. Fry over a low heat for 5 minutes or until the capsicum and onion have softened.

Add the chicken and 2 tbsp of the yogurt. Increase the heat to medium and cook for 4 minutes or until the yogurt is absorbed. Repeat with the rest of the yogurt.

Increase the heat to high, stir in the tomatoes and ¾ cup/6 fl oz/175 ml water and bring to the boil. Reduce the heat, cover, and simmer for 30 minutes or until the chicken is tender, stirring occasionally and adding more water if the sauce becomes too dry.

Uncover the pan, increase the heat to high and cook, stirring constantly, for 5 minutes or until the sauce thickens. Garnish with coriander.

# Cashew nut butter chicken

**Serves 6**

2 oz/55 g ghee or butter
2 cloves garlic, crushed
2 onions, finely chopped
1 tbsp Madras curry paste
1 tbsp ground coriander
½ tsp ground nutmeg

1 lb 13 oz/750 g boneless chicken thigh or
   breast fillets, cut into ¾ in/2 cm cubes
2 oz/55 g cashew nuts, roasted and ground
1¼ cups/½ pint/ 300 ml double
   (heavy) cream
2 tbsp coconut milk

Melt ghee or butter in a pan over medium heat, add garlic and onions and cook, stirring, for 3 minutes or until onions are golden.

Stir in curry paste, coriander and nutmeg and cook for 2 minutes or until fragrant.

Add chicken and cook, stirring, for 5 minutes or until chicken is brown.

Add cashews, cream and coconut milk, bring to simmering and simmer, stirring occasionally, for 40 minutes or until chicken is tender.

**Note:** To roast cashews, spread nuts over a baking sheet and bake at 180°C/350°F/Gas mark 4 for 5–10 minutes or until lightly and evenly browned. Turn occasionally to ensure even browning. Alternatively, place nuts under a medium grill (broiler) and cook, tossing back and forth until roasted.

# Northern Indian chicken curry

**Serves 4**

4 tbsp ghee
4 onions, sliced
2 tsp salt
1 tsp freshly ground black pepper
2 tsp sugar
1 tbsp garlic, crushed
1 tbsp fresh root ginger, crushed

2 tbsp red chillies, minced
1 bay leaf
2 tbsp garam masala
8 large chicken drumsticks
1 lb/450 g tomatoes, diced
1 tbsp tomato paste
Indian naan bread, to serve

Heat the ghee in a large pan. Stir-fry the onions until glossy. Season with salt, black pepper and sugar. Continue to stir-fry until soft but do not allow to brown.

Add the garlic, ginger, chillies, bay leaf and garam masala. Stir-fry for 1–2 minutes until spices become aromatic.

Add the chicken pieces, tomatoes and tomato paste and cook over a medium heat for about 20 minutes, adding water a little at a time, if needed. Taste and adjust seasoning with salt, pepper and sugar. Serve with Indian naan bread.

# Creamy chicken korma with rice

**Serves 4**

3 tbsp vegetable oil
1 onion, chopped
2 cloves garlic, finely chopped
3 tbsp plain (all-purpose) flour
2 tbsp mild korma curry powder
1 lb 13 oz/750 g skinless boneless chicken,
  cut into 1 in/2.5 cm cubes
12 fl oz/350 ml chicken stock

1 oz/25 g raisins
1 tbsp fresh coriander (cilantro) chopped
1 tsp/5 ml garam masala
juice of ½ lemon
4 tbsp soured cream
2 cups/14 oz/400 g steamed rice, to serve

Heat the oil in a large heavy pan, add the onion and garlic and cook gently for 5 minutes or until softened.

Put the flour and curry powder into a bowl and mix together. Toss the chicken in the seasoned flour, coating well. Reserve the flour. Add the chicken to the onion and garlic, then cook, stirring, for 3–4 minutes, until lightly browned. Stir in the seasoned flour and cook for 1 minute.

Add the stock and raisins and bring to the boil, stirring. Cover and simmer for 15 minutes.

Add the coriander and garam masala and cook for another 5 minutes or until the flavours are released and the chicken is cooked through. Remove the pan from the heat and stir in the lemon juice and soured cream. Return to the heat and warm through, taking care not to let the mixture boil. Serve with steamed rice.

**Note**: If you like curry but don't want to spend hours in the kitchen, you'll love this. It's quite mild and goes well with rice or chapattis. Try it with crispy fried onion rings.

# Mince curry with peas & mint

**Serves 6**

2¼ lb/1 kg chicken mince
1 cup/8 fl oz/250 ml cold water
2 tsp salt
2 tsp fresh garlic, crushed
2½ tsp fresh ginger, crushed
1 tsp green masala
1 tsp turmeric
2 tsp lemon juice

VAGAAR
4 tbsp/80 ml cooking oil
2 cinnamon sticks, each 2 in/5 cm
4 whole cloves

4 cardamom pods
2 onions, chopped
4 potatoes, halved
4 carrots, halved
2 tomatoes, chopped
2 tbsp coriander leaves, chopped
1 tsp garam masala
2 cups/1 lb/450 g frozen peas
3 tbsp fresh mint, chopped

In a large bowl, break up the mince thoroughly with your fingers. Add the water and stir to break up further (the water will evaporate while cooking). Mix in the salt, garlic, ginger, masala, turmeric and lemon juice.

To make the vagaar, heat the oil and spices in a large saucepan with a well-fitting lid. Add the onions, cover, reduce the heat and allow the onions to brown. Add the mince and braise for 5–7 minutes. Stir in the potatoes and carrots, then cover and cook for 30 minutes over a medium heat. Stir occasionally. Add the tomatoes, cover and cook for a further 10 minutes.

Garnish with the dhania and garam masala. Serve with warm roti, foolka bread or naan, and a dhania chutney.

Add the peas and mint to the basic mince mixture 15 minutes before the end of cooking but only after the tomatoes have been added and cooked for 10 minutes.

# Tandoori wings

**Serves 4–6**

*24 chicken wings*

*MARINADE*
*7 oz/200 g natural (plain) yogurt*
*5 tbsp tandoori paste*
*2 tbsp desiccated (dry, shredded unsweetened) coconut*
*lemon wedges, to garnish*

Combine marinade ingredients and mix well. Marinate chicken wings for at least 1 hour, ensuring each wing is well coated with the marinade.

Grill (broil) on high, turning occasionally or bake in oven on rack at 180°C/350°F/gas mark 4 for 20–25 minutes. Garnish with lemon.

# Easy chicken curry

**Serves 4–5**

*3 lb/1.3 kg chicken, jointed*
*2 oz/55 g leek and potato soup mix*
*1 tbsp curry powder*
*zest of ½ lemon, grated (shredded)*
*9 oz/250 g green beans, blanched*
*salt and freshly ground black pepper*

Trim chicken pieces and place in slow cooker. Combine soup mix and curry powder and sprinkle over and around chicken pieces. Pour over enough water to barely cover chicken and cook on high for approximately 4 hours or on low for approximately 6 hours.

About 1 hour before serving, stir in lemon zest and beans. Add salt and pepper to taste. Serve with cooked rice.

# Green chicken curry with lemongrass rice

**Serves 6**

2 cups/16 fl oz/475 ml coconut milk
1 cup/8 fl oz/250 ml chicken stock
2 tbsp green curry paste
3 kaffir lime leaves, shredded
7 oz/200 g pumpkin, chopped
4 chicken breast fillets, cubed
4 oz/115 g canned bamboo shoots, drained
4 oz/115 g snake beans (Chinese long
    beans/asparagus beans), chopped

7 oz/200 g choi sum, chopped
1 tbsp fish sauce (nam pla)
1 tbsp grated (shredded) palm sugar
¼ cup fresh Thai basil leaves, torn

LEMONGRASS RICE
1½ cups/10 oz/275 g jasmine rice
2 stalks lemongrass, bruised

Combine coconut milk, stock, curry paste and lime leaves in a slow cooker on high. Cook until the sauce begins to thicken. Add the pumpkin and cook for 20 minutes or until it starts to soften.

Add the chicken and bamboo shoots and cook for 1 hour. Add the beans, broccoli, fish sauce and palm sugar and cook until the vegetables are tender, approximately 1 more hour. Stir through the basil leaves.

To make the lemongrass rice, put the rice, lemongrass and 4 cups/ 1¾ pints/1 l water in a pan. Bring to the boil and cook over a high heat until steam holes appear in the top of the rice. Reduce the heat to low, cover and cook for 10 minutes or until all the liquid is absorbed and the rice is tender. Remove the lemongrass. Serve curry spooned over bowls of rice.

# Curried chicken wings

**Serves 4**

9 oz/250 g potatoes, peeled
1 lb 13 oz/750 g chicken wings
1 tbsp plain (all-purpose) flour
1 tbsp curry powder
1 tbsp vegetable oil
1 white onion, chopped
1 cup/8 fl oz/250 ml chicken stock
salt and freshly ground black pepper
9 oz/250 g carrots, peeled and sliced diagonally
6 spring onions (scallions), chopped (optional)

Parboil potatoes, cube roughly and set aside.

Wipe the chicken wings with absorbent paper and roll in the combined flour and curry powder. Heat the oil in a frying pan, brown the chicken, then place it in slow cooker set on low.

Add onion to frying pan and cook until softened, then add to slow cooker. Add the stock to the frying pan, stirring constantly until it boils and thickens. Season to taste and pour into slow cooker.

Add potatoes and carrots to cooker and cook for approximately 4 hours, testing after that time. Do not allow to overcook, as meat will fall from bones. Stir in spring onions, if using, just before serving. Serve curry with pappadams.

# Masala duck curry

**Serves 4**

*1 tbsp sesame oil*
*4½ lb/2 kg duck, cleaned and cut into 8 pieces*
*1 onion, chopped*
*2 small fresh red chillies, finely chopped, plus 2 sliced*
*1 stalk fresh lemongrass, bruised*
*2 tbsp green masala paste*
*1½ cups/12 fl oz/350 ml coconut milk*
*3 fresh or dried curry leaves*
*1 tbsp lime juice*
*1 tbsp brown sugar*
*¼ cup coriander (cilantro) leaves, chopped*
*1 oz/30 g fresh basil leaves*
*3 fresh green chillies, seeded and sliced*

Heat the oil in a pan over medium heat. Add duck and cook, turning frequently, for 10 minutes or until brown on all sides. Remove and drain on kitchen paper.

Add onion, chopped red chillies and lemongrass to pan and cook, stirring, for 3 minutes or until onion is golden. Stir in masala paste and cook for 2 minutes longer or until fragrant.

Stir in coconut milk, curry leaves, lime juice and sugar and return duck to pan. Bring to boil and simmer, stirring occasionally, for 45 minutes.

Add coriander, basil and sliced green and red chillies and cook for 10 minutes longer or until duck is tender. Remove lemongrass, then serve duck with green beans and rice.

# Indian salad of spiced chicken & dhal

**Serves 6–8**

7½ cups/3 pints/1.75 l vegetable stock
1½ cups/12 oz/350 g dried lentils
juice of 2 lemons
2 tbsp vegetable oil
1 tbsp curry powder
1 tbsp garam masala
1 tsp turmeric
salt and freshly ground black pepper

4 large chicken breast fillets, skin removed
1 small cauliflower, cut into florets
1½ cups/12 oz/350 g fresh or frozen peas
2 small tomatoes, deseeded and diced
1 cucumber, peeled and diced
2 spring onions (scallions), sliced
¼ cup fresh mint, chopped
2 large bunches watercress, trimmed

Bring 6 cups of vegetable stock to the boil and add the lentils. Simmer until tender, about 20 minutes. Drain, then to a large bowl and add the lemon juice and 1 tbsp of the oil. Mix well, cover and chill.

Combine the curry powder, garam masala, turmeric, salt and pepper in a plastic bag. Add the chicken, seal the bag and shake vigorously, allowing the spices to coat the chicken. Heat a frying pan with the remaining oil until smoking then add the chicken and fry until cooked through and golden on both sides, about 5 minutes. Remove the chicken and set aside.

To the same pan, add the remaining stock and bring to the boil. Add the cauliflower and peas and cook over high heat until vegetables are crisp-tender and most of the liquid has evaporated, about 5 minutes. Add this vegetable mixture to the lentils and mix well. Add the tomatoes, cucumber, spring onions and fresh mint and mix well. Season to taste.

Slice the chicken into diagonal strips then gently mix these into the salad. Arrange the watercress on a platter and top with the salad mixture, arranging so that there is plenty of chicken visible. Garnish with extra mint.

# Meat

# Beef keema

**Serves 4**

*3 tbsp vegetable oil*
*2 onions, sliced*
*1 clove garlic, crushed*
*½ in/1 cm piece fresh root ginger, finely grated (shredded)*
*1¼ lb/500 g lean beef mince*
*¼ cup fresh coriander (cilantro), chopped*
*1 fresh red chilli, chopped*
*¼ cup/2 fl oz/55 g natural (plain) yogurt*
*2 cups/14 oz/400 g brown rice*
*4 cups/1¾ pints/1 litre beef stock*
*2 whole cloves*
*1 cinnamon stick*

Heat oil in a frying pan over a medium heat. Add onions, garlic and ginger and cook, stirring, for 3–4 minutes or until onions are golden and tender. Add beef and cook, stirring, for 5 minutes or until beef is well browned.

Stir coriander, chilli and yogurt into beef mixture and cook for 1 minute. Remove pan from heat.

Place rice, stock, cloves and cinnamon stick in a large pan and bring to the boil over a medium heat. Reduce heat to simmering, cover and simmer for 45 minutes. Remove pan from heat and stand, covered, for 5 minutes.

Lightly fork onion and beef mixture through rice and heat over a low heat, stirring, for 4–5 minutes, until keema is heated through.

# Creamy veal curry

**Serves 4**

*1 tbsp vegetable oil*
*1¼ lb 500 g stewing veal, cubed and trimmed*
*1 large white onion, sliced*
*½ clove garlic, crushed or chopped*
*1 tsp curry powder*
*1 large red capsicum (bell pepper), sliced*
*2 bay leaves*
*¾ cup/6 fl oz/175 ml chicken or veal stock*
*½ cup/4 fl oz/120 ml fresh coconut milk or ¼ cup/2 fl oz/ 50 ml canned coconut cream*

Heat the oil in a large frying pan and brown the veal. Add onion and garlic and sauté, then add the curry powder and cook gently for a few minutes, stirring occasionally.

Transfer veal mixture to slow cooker and add capsicum, bay leaves and stock. Cook on low for approximately 6 hours.

About half an hour before serving, stir in coconut milk or cream. Remove bay leaves and serve with cooked rice, garnished with coriander or parsley.

# Fruity beef curry

**Serves 4**

*1¼ lb/500 g beef, cubed*
*1 large cooking apple, peeled and diced*
*4 oz/115 g dried apricots, chopped*
*¼ cup/2 oz/55 g sultanas (golden raisins) or currants*
*1 strip orange zest*
*salt and freshly ground black pepper*
*½ in/1 cm piece fresh root ginger, grated*
*1 tbsp lemon juice*
*½ clove garlic, crushed*
*1 cup/8 fl oz/250 ml beef stock*
*1–2 tbsp curry powder*
*2 tbsp natural (plain) yogurt*

Place beef in slow cooker with apple, apricots, sultanas or currants, orange zest, salt and pepper to taste, ginger, lemon juice and garlic.

Blend stock with curry powder, add to cooker and stir gently. Cook on low for approximately 6–8 hours or on high for 5–6 hours (time will vary depending on the meat). About 30 minutes before serving, stir in yogurt and heat through. Serve with rice and chutney.

If preferred, beef may be browned first in a frying pan in a little oil. This improves the flavour and colour of the dish, but is not essential.

# Lamb & spinach curry

**Serves 4**

2 tbsp vegetable oil
2 onions, chopped
2 cloves garlic, chopped
1 in/2.5 cm piece ginger, finely chopped
1 cinnamon stick
¼ tsp ground cloves
3 cardamom pods
1 lb 13 oz/750 g lamb, diced

1 tbsp ground cumin
1 tbsp ground coriander
⅓ cup natural (plain) yogurt
2 tbsp tomato paste
¾ cup/8 fl oz/250 ml beef stock
salt and freshly ground black pepper
4 oz/120 g baby spinach, chopped
2 tbsp blanched almonds, toasted

Heat the oil in a large heavy pan. Add onions, garlic, ginger, cinnamon, cloves and cardamom and cook for 5 minutes. Add the lamb and cook for 5 minutes, turning, until it begins to brown.

Transfer mixture to slow cooker set on high. Mix in the cumin and coriander, then add the yogurt 1 tbsp at a time, stirring well after each addition. Mix the tomato paste and stock together and add to the cooker. Season to taste, then reduce the heat to low and cook for 7 hours.

Stir in the spinach, cover and simmer for another 15 minutes or until the mixture has reduced slightly. Remove the cinnamon stick and the cardamom pods and mix in the almonds. Serve with rice.

# Indian meatballs in tomato sauce

**Serves 4**

1 ¼ lb/500 g lean lamb mince
½ cup/4 fl oz/120 ml natural (plain)
   yogurt
2 in/5 cm piece fresh root ginger, grated
   (shredded)
1 green chilli, deseeded, finely chopped
¼ cup chopped fresh coriander (cilantro)
2 tsp ground cumin

2 tsp ground coriander
salt and freshly ground black pepper
2 tbsp olive oil
1 onion, chopped
2 cloves garlic, chopped
½ tsp ground turmeric
1 tsp garam masala
14 oz/400 g can chopped tomatoes

Combine the lamb, 1 tablespoon yogurt, ginger, chilli, 2 tbsp of chopped coriander, cumin and ground coriander in a large bowl and season with salt and pepper. Shape the mixture into 16 balls.

Heat 1 tbsp of oil in a large pan, add meatballs and cook for 10 minutes, turning until browned (you may have to cook them in batches). Drain on kitchen paper and set aside.

In a slow cooker on a high setting add the remaining olive oil, onion and garlic and stir. Mix the turmeric and garam masala with 1 tbsp water, then add to onion and garlic. Add remaining yogurt, 1 tbsp at a time, stirring well after each addition.

Add the tomatoes, meatballs and 5 fl oz/170 ml to the mixture and bring to temperature. Cook for 5 hours, stirring occasionally. Sprinkle over the rest of the coriander to garnish and serve on a bed of rice.

# Keema curry

**Serves 4**

1 tbsp vegetable oil
1 onion, finely chopped
1 in/2.5 cm piece fresh root ginger, grated
  (shredded)
2 cloves garlic, crushed
1¼ lb/500 g lean minced lamb, at room
  temperature
2 tsp ground turmeric
1 tsp chilli powder

1 tbsp garam masala
3 tbsp tomato purée
¾ pint/450 ml lamb stock
4 oz/115 g frozen petits pois
salt and black pepper
2 tbsp chopped fresh coriander (cilantro),
  plus extra to garnish
basmati rice, cucumber raita and mango
  chutney to serve

Heat the oil in a large heavy frying pan. Add the onion and ginger and cook over a low heat for 5 minutes or until softened. Add the garlic and minced lamb, breaking the mince up with a wooden spoon. Cook for 10 minutes or until the lamb browns.

Pour off any excess fat from the pan. Add the turmeric, chilli, garam masala and tomato purée, then stir-fry for 1–2 minutes. Add the stock and bring to the boil, stirring, then reduce the heat and simmer, uncovered, for 10 minutes or until slightly reduced.

Add the petits pois, then simmer for 5–10 minutes longer. Remove from the heat, stir in the coriander and season. Garnish with extra coriander and serve with basmati rice, cucumber raita and mango chutney.

**Note**: This is a really easy way to turn minced lamb into a delicious spicy curry. It's best served the traditional way – with basmati rice, cucumber raita and mango chutney.

# Lamb curry

**Serves 6**

1¾ lb/1 kg boneless lamb
2 tbsp curry powder
1 tbsp olive oil
2 apples, peeled and diced
2 onions, chopped
¾ in/2 cm fresh root ginger, grated (shredded)
2 tbsp plain (all-purpose) flour
2 cloves garlic, crushed
1 cup/8 fl oz/250 ml dry red wine
1 cup/8 fl oz/250 ml beef stock
1 tsp lemon juice
salt and freshly ground black pepper
¼ cup fresh parsley, chopped

In a large heavy frying pan, brown meat and curry powder in olive oil.
Transfer to the slow cooker.

Add apples, onions, ginger and flour to the frying pan and cook until glazed.
Transfer to slow cooker.

Add garlic, wine, stock, lemon juice, salt and pepper and mix well. Cover
and cook on low for 8–10 hours. Serve over steamed rice and garnish
with parsley.

# Madras curry

**Serves 4**

*1 oz/30 g plain (all-purpose) flour*
*salt and freshly ground black pepper to taste*
*1¼ lb/500 g stewing steak, cubed*
*2 oz/55 g ghee or 4 tbsp oil*
*2 onions, finely chopped*
*1 tsp ground turmeric*
*1 tsp ground coriander*
*1 tsp cayenne pepper*
*½ tsp ground black mustard seeds*
*½ tsp ground cumin*
*2 cloves garlic, crushed*
*¼ pint/145 ml hot water*

Place flour in a plastic bag and season with salt and pepper. Add stewing steak, close bag and shake until evenly coated.

Heat ghee or oil in a heavy pan, add floured beef cubes and fry for 5 minutes, stirring and turning meat so that all sides are browned.

Add onions and cook, stirring occasionally, for 5 minutes longer.

Stir in spices and cook for 3 minutes, then add garlic. Cook for 2 minutes. Add the hot water. Bring to the boil and boil briskly, stirring constantly, for 5 minutes.

Stir in raisins and add more water, if necessary, to cover meat. Bring to the boil, lower heat and simmer for 2¼ hours, adding more water as required. Serve at once or cool swiftly, refrigerate and reheat next day.

# Lamb korma

**Serves 4–6**

*3½ lb/1½ kg shoulder of lamb*
*salt and freshly ground black pepper*
*2 tbsp ghee*
*1 red onion, finely chopped*
*1 clove garlic, finely chopped*
*1 tbsp green masala paste*
*¼ tsp ground ginger*
*¼ tsp turmeric*
*⅛ tsp cayenne pepper*
*2 tbsp plain (all-purpose) flour*
*1¼ cups/½ pint/300 ml chicken stock*
*¾ cup/6 oz/175 g sultanas (golden raisins)*
*¼ pint/145 ml natural (plain)yogurt*
*1 tbsp lemon juice*
*rice and sambals, to serve*

Cut lamb from bone and chop into 1¾ in/4 cm cubes. Season with salt and pepper.

Heat ghee in a large, heavy pan, add one third of the lamb and brown well on all sides. Remove and brown remainder in two batches.

Add onion and garlic and sauté until transparent. Stir in curry paste, spices and flour and cook for 1 minute. Add chicken stock, sultanas and lamb. Cover with a lid and simmer gently for 1 hour or until lamb is very tender. Stir occasionally during cooking.

Stir in yogurt and lemon juice. Serve with boiled rice and sambals.

# Pork vindaloo

**Serves 4**

1¼ lb/500 g lean pork, cubed
pinch of salt
3 small dried red chillies
1 tsp cumin seeds
1½ tsp coriander seeds
2 cloves
6 black peppercorns

1 in/2.5 cm cinnamon stick
1 in/2.5 cm fresh root ginger, grated
  (shredded)
2 cloves garlic, chopped
3 tbsp vinegar
3 tbsp oil
2 onions, finely chopped

Place pork in a pan with salt. Pour in water to cover meat by about 1 in/ 2.5 cm. Bring to the boil, lower heat and simmer for 45 minutes or until meat is tender.

Meanwhile, dry-fry chillies, cumin seeds, coriander seeds, cloves, peppercorns and cinnamon stick in a frying pan for a few minutes, until mixture starts to crackle. Don't let it burn.

Using a mortar and pestle, or a coffee grinder kept especially for the purpose, grind spices with ginger, garlic and vinegar to a smooth paste.

Heat oil in a large frying pan. Fry onions for about 10 minutes, until golden. Stir in spice paste and fry for 2 minutes more, stirring constantly.

Drain meat and reserve the cooking liquid, then add the pork to the frying pan. Stir well, cover and cook for 10 minutes over moderate heat. Add about 2 cups of reserved cooking liquid. Stir well, cover and cook for 15–20 minutes more, or until meat is coated in a thick spicy sauce.

Serve garnished with red chillies, or tip into a casserole, cool quickly, and refrigerate for reheating next day.

# Lamb soup

**Serves 6**

1¾ oz/50 g butter
1¾ lb/1 kg lamb fillet, chopped
4½ oz/115 g split red lentils, washed
4½ oz/115 g green lentils, washed
4½ oz/115 g yellow split peas, soaked
   overnight
2 onions, chopped
14 oz/400 g can chopped tomatoes
7 oz/200 g pumpkin, peeled and chopped
2 potatoes, peeled and chopped
14 oz/400 g eggplant (aubergine), finely
   chopped
1 tsp ground coriander

1 tsp ground cumin
1 tsp garam masala
½ tsp ground turmeric
1 tsp chilli powder
4 red chillies, deseeded and chopped
12 fresh mint leaves, chopped
½ cup fresh coriander (cilantro) leaves
1 in/2.5 cm piece fresh root ginger, grated
   (shredded)
4 cloves garlic, finely chopped
1 oz/30 g shredded coconut
salt and freshly ground black pepper

Heat the butter in a heavy pan and fry the lamb in small quantities until brown on all sides.

Put all other ingredients into the pan with the lamb and 12 cups water. Bring to the boil, turn down the heat and cook for 2½ hours.

Serve with pappadams and boiled rice.

# Kelapa lamb curry

**Serves 4–6**

1 tbsp olive oil
1 onion, chopped
1 tsp garlic, freshly crushed
1 tsp ginger, freshly chopped
1 tsp ground cumin
1 tsp ground coriander
1 tsp garam masala
1 tsp chilli powder
1 lb 13 oz/750 g lean lamb, cubed
½ cup/4 fl oz/120 ml coconut cream
½ cup/4 oz/115 g sultanas (golden raisins)
14 oz/400 g can mango slices, undrained
2 large bananas, chopped
Rice and pappadams to serve

Heat oil in large pan, fry onion, garlic and ginger. Add spices and fry for 1 minute.

Add lamb and fry for 2–3 minutes. Reduce heat to low, add coconut cream, sultanas and canned mangoes.

Cover and simmer for 90 minutes, stirring occasionally. Add bananas during the last 20 minutes of cooking.

Serve curry with rice and pappadams.

# Smoky lamb & eggplant soup

**Serves 6-8**

1 ¾ lb/1 kg eggplant (aubergines)
3 oz/85 g ghee or butter
2 large leeks
1 ¼ lb/500 g sweet potato, peeled
    and cubed
2 tsp ground cumin

2 tsp ground cinnamon
3 ½ lb/2 kg lamb shanks
4 cups/1 ¾ pints/1 l beef stock
4 sprigs thyme
3 cinnamon sticks
1 cup flat-leaf parsley, chopped

Prick the eggplants all over and place them on a grill (broiler) or barbecue, turning often until charred and deflated. Alternatively, bake at 220°C/425°F/ Gas mark 7 for 1 hour until the eggplants are soft and deflated. Chop the eggplant, discarding any very tough or charred skin.

Heat half the ghee or butter in a large pan, add the leeks and sauté until golden. Add the chopped eggplant, sweet potato, cumin and ground cinnamon and stir thoroughly while cooking for 5 minutes or until all the ingredients are golden and fragrant. Place this mixture in a bowl and set aside.

In the used pan, heat the remaining ghee or butter and add the lamb shanks, cooking them over a medium-high heat until they are golden all over. Add the beef stock, thyme, cinnamon sticks and 6 cups water and simmer for 1 hour.

Remove the shanks and, to the remaining soup, add the eggplant mixture and half the parsley. Simmer for 10 minutes. Meanwhile, cut all the meat off the lamb shanks and return this meat to the soup. Discard the bones.

Remove and discard the cinnamon sticks and thyme sprigs, then reheat the soup until simmering. Season to taste with salt and pepper. Stir well then serve with the remaining parsley and black pepper.

# Seafood

# Goan seafood curry

**Serves 6**

1¼ lb/500 g tiger prawns (shrimp)
9 oz/250 g firm fish
6 crayfish tails
2 tsp salt
1 tsp turmeric
1 tsp paprika (or chilli powder)
1 tsp lemon juice
1 tsp cooking oil
2 tbsp desiccated (dry, unsweetened
  shredded) coconut
6 large ripe tomatoes, skinned
3 tbsp ghee
2 tbsp cooking oil

2 large onions, finely chopped
2 tsp fresh garlic, pounded
1 tsp fresh ginger, pounded
10 curry leaves
1 tsp red chilli powder or paprika
½ tsp turmeric
1–2 green chillies, sliced lengthwise
1 tsp aniseed, crushed
2 tsp sugar
3 tbsp coriander (cilantro) leaves, chopped
2 tbsp tomato paste
1 cup/8 fl oz/250 ml coconut cream or
  single (light) cream

Rinse the prawns in cold water. Remove the heads and pinch off the claws. De-vein the prawns. Cut the fish into 2 in/5 cm pieces, sprinkle with salt and wash with cold water. Clean the crayfish tails similarly and de-vein them. Leave the bright shells on. Place the seafood in a bowl and rub in 1 tsp salt, turmeric and paprika. Add lemon juice and oil, then leave to rest for 1 hour.

Soak the coconut in 1 cup/8 fl oz/250 ml warm water. Cut the tomatoes into wedges. Heat the ghee and cooking oil in a large pan. Fry the onions until brown. Add the garlic, ginger and pinch of salt, then stir for 2 minutes. Stir in the coconut with the water. Add the curry leaves, chilli powder, turmeric, green chillies, aniseed, sugar and 2 tbsp of the coriander leaves. Cook, covered, for 15 minutes.

Stir in the tomato paste. Cook for another 15 minutes to reduce the sauce. (Cook until the oil rises to the surface in small bubbles.) Stir in the cream. Gently add the seafood, cover, and leave to simmer for another 15 minutes. Garnish with the remaining coriander, and serve with rice, salad and a tomato relish or yogurt.

# Spiced fish

**Serves 6**

1¾ lbs/1 kg fresh fish, filleted and sliced
2 medium tomatoes, sliced
2 medium onions, cut into rings

MARINADE
1 tsp red masala
3 tsp coriander-cumin
1 tsp fresh garlic, crushed

1 tsp turmeric
1 tbsp lemon juice
2 tbsp cooking oil
2 tsp salt
2 tbsp fresh coriander (cilantro)
  leaves, chopped
Rice or mashed potatoes, salad, rolls and
  pickles, to serve

Wash the fish and dry with kitchen paper.

Combine the marinade ingredients and rub the paste over the slices of fish.
Place in a non-metallic ovenproof dish and leave to marinate for
1–2 hours.

Regularly basting with the marinade, cook the fish under a grill (broiler) for
7 minutes. Add the tomatoes and onions and grill for another 7 minutes or
until the vegetables are soft.

Serve with rice or mashed potato, a tossed salad, rolls and pickles.

# Curried scallops

**Serves 6**

*8 oz/250 g scallops*
*½ cup/4 fl oz/120 ml dry white wine*
*1 bouquet garni*
*4 oz/115 g butter*
*1¼ cups/8 fl oz/250 ml single (light) cream*
*½ tsp curry powder*
*salt and freshly ground black pepper*
*2 egg yolks*
*2 tbsp milk*

Place scallops, white wine and bouquet garni in the slow cooker and cook on low for approximately 1 hour. Pour off and reserve liquid, discard bouquet garni and keep scallops warm in slow cooker.

Put cooking liquid with butter into a small pan and boil hard to reduce. Stir in the cream, curry powder and salt and pepper, and again boil hard for 2–3 minutes. Remove from heat and allow to cool.

Beat egg yolks with milk, and carefully stir into cooled cream mixture. Pour mixture back into slow cooker with the scallops and cook on high for 45–60 minutes. To serve, place a little cooked rice in a small bowl and spoon over 3–4 scallops with a generous quantity of sauce. Serve immediately.

# Goan curry with clams & raita

**Serves 4**

1 tsp oil
1 onion, finely sliced
2 cloves garlic, chopped
1 tbsp ground cumin
1 tbsp ground turmeric
2 tbsp mild curry powder
1 tbsp ground ginger
2 cardamom pods, cracked
pinch of chilli powder
¼ stick cinnamon
2½ lb/1 kg clams, cleaned and
  sand removed

1½ cups/12 fl oz/275 ml coconut cream
¼ cup fresh coriander (cilantro)
  leaves, chopped

RAITA
½ cucumber, peeled, seeds removed, then
  diced
¼ cup mint, chopped
5 tbsp natural (plain) yogurt
juice of 1 lemon
salt and freshly ground black pepper

On medium heat in a large pan, add oil, onion, garlic and all spices, and cook gently for 2 minutes. Add shellfish and ½ cup water, and cook until shellfish have opened, stirring frequently. As shellfish are opening, add coconut cream and coriander leaves.

To make raita, mix all ingredients together. Remove cinnamon and serve curry in a large bowl with basmati rice and garnished with raita.

# Goan-style fish & coconut curry

**Serves 4**

2 tomatoes
2 cardamom pods, husks discarded and
  seeds reserved
1 tsp each of ground coriander, cumin,
  cinnamon and hot chilli powder
½ tsp ground turmeric
2 tbsp water
2 tbsp vegetable oil
1 onion, finely chopped

1 clove garlic, finely chopped
1 in/2.5 cm piece fresh root ginger, finely
  chopped
14 fl oz/400 ml can coconut milk
1½ lb/675 g skinless white fish fillet,
  such as haddock or cod, cut into 1 in/
  2.5 cm chunks
salt, to taste
fresh coriander (cilantro) to garnish

Place tomatoes in a bowl, cover with boiling water and leave to stand for 30 seconds. Peel, then finely dice flesh.

Crush cardamom seeds using a mortar and pestle. Add coriander, cumin, cinnamon, chilli powder, turmeric and water and mix to a paste. Set aside.

Heat oil in a large, heavy pan. Fry onion, garlic and ginger for 3 minutes or until softened. Add spice paste, mix well and fry for 1 minute, stirring constantly.

Pour in coconut milk and bring to the boil, stirring. Reduce heat and simmer for 10 minutes or until liquid has reduced slightly. Add fish, tomatoes and salt. Partly cover pan and simmer, stirring occasionally, for another 10 minutes or until fish turns opaque and is cooked through. Garnish with coriander.

**Note**: Cook any favourite white fish in this spicy sauce and take your taste buds on a journey to southern India. You'll need plenty of rice to soak up the coconut sauce.

# Chilli sesame prawn kebabs

**Serves 6**

1 tbsp vegetable oil
1 tbsp Madras curry paste
2 tbsp fresh ginger, grated (shredded)
2 cloves garlic, crushed
2 tbsp lime juice
½ cup/4 oz/115 g natural (plain) yogurt
36 uncooked medium prawns (shrimp),
   shelled and deveined, tails intact

6 tbsp sesame seeds, toasted

GREEN MASALA ONIONS
1 oz/30 g ghee or butter
2 onions, cut into wedges
2 tbsp hreen Masala paste

Place oil, curry paste, ginger, garlic, lime juice and yogurt in a bowl and mix to combine. Add prawns and toss to coat. Cover and marinate in the refrigerator for 2–3 hours.

Drain prawns and thread three prawns onto an oiled skewer. Repeat with remaining prawns to make twelve kebabs. Toss kebabs in sesame seeds and cook on a lightly oiled, preheated medium barbecue or under a grill (broiler) for 3 minutes each side or until prawns are cooked.

To make masala onions, melt ghee or butter in a pan over a medium heat, add onions and cook, stirring, for 5 minutes or until soft. Stir in masala paste and cook for 2 minutes longer or until heated through. Serve with prawns.

# Curry mussels

**Serves 4**

*2 tbsp olive oil*
*1 small onion, chopped*
*1 stalk celery, sliced*
*1 clove garlic, chopped*
*2 tbsp yellow curry paste*
*2 cardamom pods, crushed*
*pinch of ground cumin*
*2½ lb/1 kg mussels, cleaned*
*¼ cup/2 fl oz/55 ml coconut cream*
*¼ cup fresh coriander (cilantro), chopped*
*1 red chilli, chopped, optional*

Put oil, onion, celery, garlic, curry paste, cardamom and cumin in a pan and cook over a slow heat for 5 minutes, stirring frequently.

Add mussels and coconut cream and increase heat to high. Cook until all mussels have opened, stirring frequently to ensure mussels are cooked evenly. Discard any mussels that do not open.

Add coriander, stir and serve. Add chopped chilli if you like your curry very spicy.

# Desserts

# Indian pistachio dumplings

**Serves 4**

pinch salt
2 tbsp sunflower oil
8 oz/225 g rice flour
5 oz/150 g sugar
3½ oz/100 g coconut, grated (shredded), if
  fresh, or desiccated (dry, unsweetened
  shredded)

3½ oz/100 g unsalted pistachios,
  crushed finely
1 tsp ground cardamom
4 tbsp ghee, warmed

Bring ¾ cup/½ pint/300 ml of water to the boil in a pan and add the salt and the oil. Reduce the heat and add the rice flour, stirring constantly until a ball is formed. Remove from the heat and leave until cool enough to handle, then knead into a soft pliable dough.

To make a sugar syrup, heat the sugar and a dash of water until sugar has dissolved. Add the coconut and pistachios. Stir for 1 minute, then remove from the heat. Add the cardamom powder and 2 tablespoons of water and combine well.

Make small balls of the dough. Take a ball of dough in your palm and flatten it into a disc. Place a portion of the coconut mixture in the middle of the disc and fold up the edges to make a dumpling. Form the dumplings into large teardrop shapes.

Steam the dumplings for 20 minutes or until done. Serve drizzled with hot ghee.

# Orange, cardamom & lime cheesecake

**Serves 4**

5 oz/150 g plain sweet biscuits (cookies),
    finely crushed
3 oz/90 g butter, melted

FILLING
7 oz/200 g cream cheese (farmer's cheese),
    softened
½ tsp ground cardamom
2 tbsp brown sugar
zest of 1 orange

zest of 2 limes
3 tsp orange juice
3 tsp lime juice
1 egg, lightly beaten
½ cup/4 fl oz/120 ml sweetened
    condensed milk
2 tbsp double (heavy) cream, whipped
2 tbsp desiccated (dry, unsweetened
    shredded) coconut, toasted, to decorate

Combine biscuits and butter in a bowl and mix to combine. Press mixture over base and sides of a well-oiled 9 in/23 cm springform tin (pan). Refrigerate to set. Preheat oven to 180°C/350°F/Gas mark 4.

Place cream cheese, cardamom, sugar, orange and lime zest and juices in a mixing bowl and beat until creamy. Beat in egg, then mix in condensed milk and fold in cream.

Spoon mixture into prepared base and bake for 25–30 minutes or until just firm. Turn oven off and allow cheesecake to cool in oven with door ajar. Leave to go cold, then chill before serving. Serve decorated with toasted coconut.

# Indian yogurt banana cake

**Serves 6**

3 oz/85 g desiccated (dry, unsweetened shredded) coconut, toasted
4½ oz/125 g ghee or clarified butter
5 oz/150 g caster (superfine) sugar
1¾ oz/40 g brown sugar
2 eggs
3 very ripe bananas

7 oz/200 g Greek (strained plain) yogurt
9 oz/250 g self-raising (self-rising) flour
1 tsp cinnamon
½ tsp mixed spice (apple pie spice)
7 oz/200 g sour cream or crème fraîche
3½ oz/100 g icing (confectioner's) sugar
1¾ oz/50 g toasted shredded coconut

Preheat the oven to 190°C/375°/Gas mark 5. Line the base of a 8–10 in/ 22–24 cm non-stick springform tin (pan) with baking parchment. Grease the sides and pour in the toasted coconut. Tip the tin all around to coat the greased sides with the coconut, then pour out the excess and reserve for the cake batter.

Beat the ghee and sugars in a bowl until creamy, then add the eggs, one at a time, beating well after each addition.

Mash the bananas and add to the ghee/sugar mixture with the yogurt, flour, cinnamon, spice and remaining coconut and stir to combine with a wooden spoon. Tip the mixture into the prepared tin and smooth the top.

Bake 55 minutes, or until firm and 'springy' when touched in the centre. Remove from the oven, allow to cool for 15 minutes, then remove the sides of the tin and cool completely. Remove the base and baking paper and place on a platter.

To make the icing, mix together the sour cream and icing sugar until thick and spreadable, then spread over the top of the cool cake. Pour the shredded coconut over the cream, until thickly covered.

# Indian carrot cake

**Serves 4**

4 large eggs
1 tsp ground cardamom
1 tsp mixed spice (apple pie spice)
¼ tsp ground cloves
1 lb/450 g sugar
3½ oz/100 g ghee, softened, or
    vegetable oil, plus extra for greasing
7 oz/200 g carrots, grated (shredded)
zest of 1 orange

½ cup/2 oz/55 g pistachio nuts, chopped
    and toasted
½ cup/2 oz/55 g cashew nuts, chopped
    and toasted
½ cup/4 oz/115 g sultanas (golden
    raisins)
230 g self-raising (self-rising) flour
icing (confectioner's) sugar, for dusting

Preheat the oven to 180°C/350°G/Gas mark 4. Grease a large non-stick loaf tin (pan), then dust it lightly with some of the flour. Set aside.

In a large bowl, mix together the eggs, cardamom, mixed spice, ground cloves, sugar and ghee and whisk until the batter is smooth. Add the carrots, orange zest, nuts and sultanas, then add the flour, mixing to combine.

Pour the batter into the prepared tin and bake for 45 minutes, or until the top of the cake is golden brown and 'springy' when pressed gently in the centre. Remove the cake from the oven and allow to set for a few minutes, then turn out onto a wire rack to go cold.

Dust with icing sugar before serving.

# Indian rice pudding with pistachios

**Serves 4**

2 oz/55 g basmati rice
¾ pint/450 ml whole milk
14 oz/400 g can evaporated milk
butter, for greasing
3 cardamom pods, husks discarded and seeds reserved
1 cinnamon stick
2 oz/55 g caster (superfine) sugar
2 tbsp flaked (slivered) almonds, toasted
1 oz/30 g shelled pistachios, roughly chopped

Preheat the oven to 150°C/300°F/Gas mark 2. Place the rice, milk and evaporated milk in a heavy pan and bring to a simmer, taking care not to let the mixture boil. Simmer, uncovered, for 10 minutes.

Grease an ovenproof dish. Transfer the rice mixture to the dish, then stir in the cardamom seeds, cinnamon, sugar, almonds and pistachios, reserving 1 tablespoon to decorate. Bake for 2 hours, or until reduced to a thick consistency, stirring in the skin that forms on top every 30 minutes. Remove the cinnamon stick. Serve warm or cold, topped with the reserved pistachios.

# Gulab jamun

**Serves 6**

6 oz/170 g sugar
8 green cardamom pods
1 oz/30 g self-raising (self-rising) flour
4½ oz/125 g powdered skimmed milk
1 oz/30 g ghee or butter
1 oz/30 g cream (farmer's) cheese

1–2 tbsp rosewater
2–3 tbsp milk or natural (plain) low-fat
  yogurt
oil, for deep-frying

Put 5 oz/150 g of the sugar with the 6 fl oz/175 ml water in a wide pan or deep frying-pan. Stir over gentle heat until sugar has dissolved, then add cardamom pods. Increase heat and boil for 15 minutes to make a light syrup. Reduce heat to lowest setting to keep syrup warm.

Combine flour and powdered milk in a bowl. Rub in ghee or butter, then add remaining sugar, cream cheese, rosewater and enough milk or yogurt to form a soft dough. Knead lightly and roll into 18 small balls.

Heat oil for deep-frying. Cook the dough balls in small batches, keeping them moving in the oil until they are golden brown all over. Remove with a slotted spoon and drain on kitchen paper for 5 minutes. Remove syrup from heat and add the cooked dough balls. Allow to cool to room temperature in syrup. To serve, transfer to individual plates with a slotted spoon, then add 2–3 tablespoons syrup.

**Note**: These small dumplings in a spicy syrup are a traditional dessert. They are usually made with full-fat powdered milk. This is not always easy to obtain, so this recipe uses skimmed milk powder and adds cream cheese.

# Index

Aadoo mirch  17

Bombay hot lentils 39
Bread
  Chapatis 29
  Coconut poori 33
  Indian fresh corn31
  Naan 27
  Potato naan 49
  Spicy wholemeal parathas 47

Cashew nut butter chicken 113
Chicken Tropicana 105
Chilli sesame prawn kebabs 173
Coconut sambal 55
Curried chicken wings 127
Curried scallops 167
Curry mussels 175
Curry
  Bean 61
  Beef keema 135
  Chicken rogan josh 111
  Creamy chicken korma with rice 117
  Creamy veal 137
  Easy chicken 123
  Fruity beef 139
  Goan seafood 163
  Goan with clams & raita 169
  Goan-style fish & coconut 171
  Green chicken with lemongrass rice 125
  Keema 145
  Kelapa lamb 157
  Lamb & spinach 141

Lamb 147
Lamb korma 151
Maddras 149
Masala duck 129
Mince with peas & mint 119
Northern Indian chicken 115
Pork vindaloo 153
Root vegetable 89
Spicy lentil dhal with ginger &
  coriander 57
Vegetable & lentil 67
Vegetable 87
Vegetable korma 81
curry paste, Green masala 13
  Madras 19
  Masala 18
  Vindaloo 14
  Garam masala 17

Dips
  Chickpea & eggplant  25
  Roasted red capsicum raita 45
  Spiced yogurt 53

Fresh mint chutney 71

Gulab jamun 189

Indian carrot cake 185
  chicken with spiced yellow rice 103
  meatballs in tomato sauce 143
  pancakes 35
  pistachio dumplings 179

rice pudding with pistachios 187
salad of spiced chicken & dhal 131
yogurt banana cake 183

Lentil & rice dumplings 43
Lentil burger 85

Moong sprouts 37

Orange, cardamom & lime cheesecake 181

Potato & pea bhajis 83

Red lentils 77
Rice
  Fragrant pilau rice 51
  Simple pilau rice 63
  South Indian spiced rice with green
  beans & peas 65
  Spicy yogurt rice 41
Roasted Patiala chicken breasts 107

Salad
  Chickpea with spinach 75
  Curried potato & egg 97
  Moghul 69
  Okra & chickpea 91
Soup
  Cool cumin-scented yogurt 99
  Indian curried vegetable 95
  Indian lentil 93
  Indian spiced potato & onion 73
  Lamb 155

Smoky lamb & eggplant 159
spice mix, Tandoori 15
Spiced fish 165

Tandoori wings 121
Thoor lentils 79
Tikka skewers 109

Vegetable samosas 23

First published 2013 by
New Holland Publishers Pty Ltd
London · Sydney · Cape Town · Auckland

Garfield House 86–88 Edgware Road London W2 2EA United Kingdom
1/66 Gibbes Street Chatswood NSW 2067 Australia
Wembley Square First Floor Solan Road Gardens Cape Town 8001 South Africa
218 Lake Road Northcote Auckland New Zealand

www.newhollandpublishers.com

A record of this book is held at the British Library and the National Library of Australia

ISBN  9781742573885

Publisher: Fiona Schultz
Designer: Lorena Susak
Production director: Olga Dementiev
Printer: Toppan Leefung Printing Limited

10 9 8 7 6 5 4 3 2 1

Texture: Shutterstock photo

Keep up with New Holland Publishers on Facebook http://www.facebook.com/
NewHollandPublishers

UK £9.99
US $14.99